PRAISE FOR *THE FAST AND FURIOUS FIVE-STEP ORGANIZING SOLUTION:*

"I love this book! The author's humor, wit, and efficiency are a perfect match for her fast and furious organizing ideas, and the before-and-after photographs give the reader a clear vision of how elegant and serene an organized space can be. Highly recommended!"

—Kathy Waddill, author of *The Organizing Sourcebook: Nine Strategies for Simplifying Your Life*

PAST PRAISE FOR PINSKY'S *ORGANIZING SOLUTIONS FOR PEOPLE WITH ATTENTION DEFICIT DISORDER:*

"Pinsky brings real-life experience to her topic. Not only is she a professional organizer and member of the National Association of Professional Organizers, but she is also the parent of a child with attention deficit disorder (ADD). These two roles led to her creating simplified organizational systems specific to the needs of those with ADD. The book's first section explains her organizational methods; the second targets specific areas, rooms, or events that are common to almost everyone and typically present a challenge to organize and keep organized. Pinsky uses an abundance of before-and-after color photographs as well as yellow Post-its®-styled notes to highlight tips for organization. Her organizational philosophy can apply to everyone, not just those with ADD. This book is easy to read, and the pictures clearly depict the look of organization. Highly recommended for all public libraries."

—*Library Journal*

TO ESTHER, HANNAH, AND LEAH,
FOR THEIR GOOD HUMOR THROUGH IT ALL

Text © 2010 Susan C. Pinsky
First published in the USA in 2010 by
Fair Winds Press, a member of
Quayside Publishing Group
100 Cummings Center
Suite 406-L
Beverly, MA 01915-6101
www.fairwindspress.com

14 13 12 11 10   2 3 4 5

ISBN-13: 978-1-59233-419-3
ISBN-10: 1-59233-419-9

Library of Congress Cataloging-in-Publication Data
Pinsky, Susan C.
  The fast and furious five-step organizing solution : no-fuss clutter control from a top
professional organizer / Susan C. Pinsky.
     p. cm.
  Includes index.
  ISBN-13: 978-1-59233-419-3
  ISBN-10: 1-59233-419-9
  1. Storage in the home. 2. Organization. I. Title.
  TX309.P58 2010
  648'.8—dc22
                                                        2010019117

Book and cover design by brandhamdesign.com
Photography by Eric Roth Photography

Printed and bound in China

THE FAST AND FURIOUS 5^{STEP} ORGANIZING SOLUTION

No-Fuss Clutter Control from a Top Professional Organizer

Susan C. Pinsky
Owner/Founder of Organizationally Yours

FAIR WINDS
PRESS
BEVERLY, MASSACHUSETTS

CONTENTS

INTRODUCTION

SOME YEARS AGO, I developed an expertise helping a type of client that falls within the population we professional organizers call the "chronically disorganized." I specialized in working with people who had been diagnosed with Attention Deficit Hyperactivity Disorder, or ADHD. How I organized the homes of these clients varied significantly from the usual advice and practices used by many professional organizers. Eventually I was asked to write a book on the subject. But something funny happened when the book came out. From readers to reviewers to interviewers, I was continually met with the comment, "But these practices would work for anyone!" I realized that, in fact, I had already begun using variations of these same techniques with *all* of my clients. Because these systems relied on efficiency over aesthetics, preparedness, and parsimony, they rendered any disorganized home—whether the chaos was the result of pathology or an over-stressed schedule—into a clutter-free, restful, and, most importantly, *easy to maintain* space. And because *all* of my clients preferred to spend their time enjoying themselves rather than fussing with organizing and cleaning, efficiency became our battle cry.

In this book, I have taken the methods I use for my most intractably disorganized clients and modified them ever so slightly to provide a fast and furious, no-fuss five-step system that will organize every room in any home that struggles with clutter. In an ADHD home, the emphasis is unwaveringly on efficiency; in your home, we can allow some reasonable and limited compromises that will render your space very efficient while also keeping aesthetics in mind. Where we made these compromises and how we organized the rest in real homes is the subject of this book. If you have already read *Organizing Solutions for People with ADD*, you'll recognize many of these techniques. For the rest of you, I hope that this method will reveal how simple and easy it is to organize and maintain a home in five easy steps when efficiency sits at the top of our value system.

PART 1

LEARN THE KE

> "A man is rich in proportion to the number of things which he can afford to leave alone"
>
> —Henry David Thoreau

YS TO CHANGE

THE FIVE-STEP METHOD

Living in a cluttered, disorganized space is a lot like being overweight. It's hard to move around, get dressed, get out of the house, and so on. In part one, we'll learn the five easy steps that can fast and furiously, without fuss, bring organization to any space and home, but as always, the devil is in the details. If we only learned the steps, it would be as though we said "eat less" without identifying the underlying habits and triggers that packed on all those pounds. So, too, with organizing we have to go further and identify those behaviors, systems, or bits of organizational misinformation that ambush our spaces. As we learn how to get organized in five easy steps, we'll also learn how to *stay* organized by changing our lifestyle, transforming our relationships to space and "stuff."

CHAPTER 1

WHAT IS THE FIVE-STEP METHOD?

Before

AS IT TURNS OUT, organizing is not rocket science. Even large, seemingly overwhelming projects can be quickly brought to a satisfyingly organized conclusion by relying on a no-fuss adherence to five simple steps.

After

THE FAST AND FURIOUS FIVE-STEP METHOD

1. **Plan:** Schedule your project days, find local charities, research containers, purchase garbage bags, and simplify rubbish removal.

2. **Weed and sort:** Empty the space, weeding out the unwanted into garbage bags and donation bags. Place "keeper" items that belong elsewhere into piles named for their destination (e.g., a "goes to kitchen" pile). Sort keeper items that stay in this room into piles by type (e.g., a "sweaters" pile).

3. **Remove:** Put "other areas" piles away, take donations to the car, and take the garbage out. Give the emptied space a quick cleaning.

4. **Name:** Return keeper items to named spaces within *boundaries*.

5. **Containerize:** If necessary, purchase, build, and install simple containers and arrange your things in them. On the way to the store, drop off donations and garbage to *their* appropriate containers—charity drops for the former and, if necessary, the dump or dumpster for the latter. If no purchases are necessary, then just do the charity and garbage run.

Sounds simple and even familiar, right? Much of this advice can be found in many books and articles on organizing. We're not going to waste time here reinventing the wheel; rather, we'll reexamine the journey itself.

Why, using many of these steps in the past, haven't you reached your goal of an organized home? And how can we alter your path so that this time you find your way, fast and furiously, to a *maintainable* organized space?

The answer is, we employ some common organizational methods that are sound, but we *reject* those organizational habits or values that, while traditional or even laudable, hang up our project on the shoals of perfectionism, aesthetics, or false economy. In the coming chapters, we'll review each of our five steps in depth, but first let's look briefly at those values that help and those that hurt our chances for an organized home.

ORGANIZING PRINCIPLE: THE ORGANIZED PERSON KNOWS EFFICIENCY IS THE ANSWER

As it turns out, not all organization is *good* organization; let me give you a risible example. I could organize your wardrobe by keeping all of your shirts in the attic and all of your pants in the basement. This is perfectly organized, but of course it's madly inefficient. *Good* organization gives preference to the most efficient systems—those that require *the least number of steps, the least amount of effort*.

Typically, as I go through a client's home, I find myriad inefficiencies: The good china is stored in the basement (far from where it's used or cleaned), the cupboards are packed to bursting with food (rendering most of it invisible and thus impossible to inventory), and winter coats are switched to the basement at the end of the season, rather than just left in the coat closet (where they belong). Although any one of these systems is manageable, it's the aggregate of *so many* small inefficiencies that creates the chaos. If you have to cross the room multiple times to unload your dishwasher, sort your laundry into five different cycles and temperatures, find the label maker to create a file, and run to the basement to grab the overstock of bulk shopping that doesn't fit in your kitchen, then you are *never* going to get out from underneath the clutter.

Getting organized is great, but it's worthless if we can't *stay* organized. As we learn how to organize, we're also going to learn how to, fast and furiously (which is to say, not perfectly, nor beautifully, nor parsimoniously), set up efficient, no-fuss systems that allow us to *stay* organized with minimum effort. Our goal is to *drastically reduce and eliminate* the excesses of modern life, simplify your systems, and create a home so efficient that going forward you'll be able to straighten up any room, fast and furiously, in *under* three minutes!

But be prepared, as we really look at what a fast and furious no-fuss approach to our five-step method means, you may well be shocked, even appalled. Because traditional organizing often values small and even false economies over time, space, stress, and effort, efficiency is neglected. (For instance, urging us to organize coupons though these coupons *encourage* spending and result in cluttered, overstocked storage areas!) While the fast and furious no-fuss system is very inexpensive to implement, we will nonetheless value time over insignificant sums of money. We will value simplicity over hard to maintain but beautiful systems. And because in the long run it's more efficient, we will value resourcefulness over preparedness, and slap-dash-no-fuss "get-it-done-ness" over perfectionism. We will acknowledge that if you bought a book about organizing "fast and furiously," then time may be your most precious possession and efficiency your most effective weapon.

BE WARNED—GETTING ORGANIZED FAST AND FURIOUSLY INCLUDES THE FOLLOWING:

- Rejecting perfectionism

- Getting it done

- Leaving a few non-urgent projects (such as photos) stowed away, all parts together—which is organized enough—possibly for years

- Abandoning projects that are not important, or that are no longer important, so that you can eliminate them from your space

- Learning to let go of the past and some dreams of the future in order to embrace the present

Learning to recognize the misguided values that are ambushing your space is the necessary prelude to an organized home. Our five-step method is only the sword of change; it can't battle these monsters alone. We need our fast and furious knights of slap-dash efficiency to finally slay the dragon. So let's start by looking at that beast: "Perfectionism." Let's see how doing everything perfectly means we might not get anything done at all, in other words, how "even better is the enemy of good enough." Then let's look at some fast and furious warriors that can help us rout the invasion of "too much stuff" and "too much fuss" from our homes.

ORGANIZING PRINCIPLE: THE ORGANIZED PERSON ABANDONS PERFECTIONISM

Let's review some common areas in which perfectionism can actually sabotage organization. Of course, every family will still wish to indulge in one or two inefficiencies, but go ahead and see if one, or even several, of these common perfectionist tendencies are not worth compromising the efficiency in your home

Perfectionist Pitfall #1: The Need to Be the Perfect Host/Hostess

In the photo to the right, you can see a kitchen cabinet of a typical American suburban home. This family has one regular tea drinker who typically drinks two cups of tea daily, choosing between only two favorite flavors. She lives five minutes from a grocery store that she visits weekly, yet she stocks ten boxes of tea containing twenty to forty tea bags each!.

Why? Because this tea drinker strives to be the "perfect hostess," providing variety and favorites for all of her guests.

Do you keep a full bar in case someone requests a mojito? Are you storing extra bathrobes, sweaters, toiletries, or bathing suits for out-of-town guests to use? Have you stocked your home with toys so the grandchildren will have a choice when they visit?

If your house is cluttered, there is no question that something you are doing to make your life better is instead making it worse.

If so, consider that no home can get organized by supplying every need, for every individual, and every organization all of the time. The fact is that you will never be able to provide every need for every family member or guest. Limit foods to those you imminently plan to consume and redundant toys to the number of children who live in the house, and you will forever simplify your storage.

Five Areas Commonly Ambushed by a False "Need" for Variety

1. Snack cabinet
2. Cereal cabinet
3. CD/DVD shelves
4. Stationery/office supplies
5. Crafts

The Emperor of China could serve his court for weeks with the stock of tea to be found in the average modern home.

Perfectionist Pitfall #2: The Need to Have the Complete Collection

If you're driven to "complete the collection," then perfectionism has likely ensnared you into a life of clutter. For example, do you:

- Provide your children with every book in the series before they have finished reading the first one?
- Keep your late parent's classical records, although you are a jazz lover, because they fill out your "music library"?
- Hang on to teacups and saucers, when you use only mugs, because they "belong to your set"?

In an organized home, items are retained because they are useful in your life *now*, not because they may *someday* be useful, might someday increase in value, complete a random collection, or provide a service you might never need.

Clutter breeds when we stock a "library" of choices. Some tea drinkers value the *idea* of variety even if they usually stick to one or two favorites. If our tea drinker stocked only two flavors and when they were gone, she replaced them with two more *of a different variety*, variety is maintained, but it's maintained *sequentially*. Sequential variety is efficient. Children get out of the house easier in the morning if they don't have to puzzle through more than two choices of cereals, juice boxes, or snack foods. One box of no-fuss seascape stationery can service everything from a birthday to a thank you, and the radio will provide a variety of music sequentially without having to fuss with CDs, downloading tunes, or managing backups.

Perfectionist Pitfall #3: The Need to Be "Too Clean"

A former client never removed still damp dishes from the dishwasher for fear they would warp her cupboard shelves. While they air-dried, dirty dishes accumulated on the counters and sink, rendering the kitchen unusable and foul-smelling. Others won't put lightly worn clothes they plan to wear again back in the drawer because they will "infect" the clean clothes. Ironically, these perfectionist systems of "clean" result in dirt and clutter.

Some "too-clean" habits are the result of nefarious influences. Tell me why exactly it is that our shirts must be whiter than white? That outerwear must be washed after one wearing when it is neither sweaty nor stained? Why must we whiten until our teeth glow in the dark? Why rinse *and repeat*?

Consider that modern advertising was pretty much invented by the soap companies. Profit rises when you go through their products quickly. Resist their perfectionist yammering. Instead, embrace efficiency and clean as a *response* to dirt, not as a prophylactic against it.

Perfectionist Pitfall #4: The Need for Beauty above All Else

Beauty appeals to the perfectionist in all of us, yet a system that relies primarily on beauty can sabotage efficiency. Again and again, I see magazine articles and newspaper pieces on "how to organize," but what the articles really promote, with a beauty shot, is a fussy, difficult to maintain, but attractive system. Yes, a series of rattan baskets in cubby units will look good, but that appealing uniformity "hides" your stuff. You'll forever grab the wrong basket unless you label them. (Talk about extra steps!)

The following four behaviors rely on the aesthetics of "uniformity" rather than no-fuss efficiency:

- Rewriting recipes onto pre-printed cards
- Decanting your spices into matching jars
- Repacking your groceries in plastic food storage (Tupperware-style) containers
- Fussing with label makers when a felt-tipped pen will be quicker and just as legible

When we engage in these behaviors, perfectionism has us fussing with packaging in the belief that beauty, not efficiency, is the basis for organization. Of course, not every solution fits every home. If you have vermin, then plastic food containers may be necessary, but we can all challenge our systems to see where efficiency is served and where chasing beauty is just another way of feeding the perfectionist beast.

ORGANIZING PRINCIPLE: THE ORGANIZED PERSON IS RESOURCEFUL, NOT PREPARED

Many modern families have cluttered homes not because they are lazy, but rather because they are trying so hard to "be prepared." Prudence mutates into a kind of "preparation perfectionism" that ambushes organization. When you try preparing for everything, you become so overwhelmed that, ironically, in the end, you are prepared for nothing.

A tea drinker is prepared to offer many varieties to her guests, a mother is prepared with a riding toy for every visiting child, a den leader is prepared to loan any camping supply to whichever troop may need it, an audiophile is prepared to play any music requested, a hostess has the correct service for everything from onion soup to sorbet, and a tax accountant is prepared to digitally photograph and label donation items for correct deductions. Are these very prepared people organized? Do you think their houses are uncluttered?

I can attest that this is emphatically not the case. These were my clients. I have been in their homes and many more like them, and the common denominator is that it's hard to cook in their kitchens, pull into their garages, sit in their living rooms, or pay bills in their offices.

If these clients had embraced resourcefulness, my hostess could have served both onion soup and sorbet from a cereal bowl; my accountant could have punted data-entering and photographing minor donations, giving him room and time to pay his bills; my den leader could have dumped the supplies while enabling other troops to master the scout-like attribute of self-reliance; my audiophile could have enjoyed a more limited collection or surprised himself with the selections on the radio; and my homemaker could have taught the children to share riding toys.

> When you try preparing for everything, you become so overwhelmed by the amount of stock and the intricate systems you are managing that you end up paralyzing yourself and your space.

Applying Resourcefulness

Historically, people bought less, used less, made do with less. Instead, they were resourceful with what they already had. We could—and should!—learn a lot from them.

Let's again turn to the example of one of my clients. A gourmet cook and mother of three who sold kitchenware through home parties, she had not cooked a meal in her own small kitchen in over eighteen months. A single glance revealed that the problem lay in an overstock of specialized cooking supplies (received as sales prizes). Yet when I suggested that we weed some of these gadgets, she replied that each item was unique and helpful. The skillets had ergonomic handles, the mini food processor did small dicing jobs, a "retro" apple peeler was fun, and two plastic discs scooped crumbs off the counter in a jiff.

With all these free specialty items crowding every bit of counter space in the kitchen, there was no place left to actually prepare food. Instead of being prepared with just the right tool, she needed to be resourceful with just those *few* tools her grandmother used. A sharp knife will chop an onion, core an apple, and dice almost anything. And it doesn't require disassembly to clean. (How efficient is that!)

Living Resourcefully

Resourceful living will clear your storage of clutter and simplify your life. In a home organized around resourcefulness, you will—brace yourself for a shocker—*regularly run out of staples*! The marketers would like you to believe that running out of something signifies a failure of organization; I say it is an organizational *triumph* and a necessary adjunct to a sane life. Cribbing a roll of toilet paper from another bathroom, making do with tea instead of coffee, or eating cereal instead of toast for a day or two, until the next run to the grocery store, keeps our inventory manageable, our money in our wallets (not tied up in unnecessary overstock), and simplifies our purchasing to items we truly need.

We've identified those values that help us stay organized—efficiency and resourcefulness—and rejected those that sabotage us—perfectionism and being overly prepared. In the chapters that follow, we'll look in detail at the mechanics of each of our five steps, followed in some cases by examples, similar to those above, of the common ways that each step can be ambushed.

PLAN

Day Morning	Sun	Mon	Tues	Weds	Thurs	Fri	Sat
Afternoon					gym shoes in back pack		
		Lars Chess club 4:00-5:30 5:45	Jill Lacrosse Practice 3:30-5:00 6:00				
Dinner **Evening**	7:15					Jill Lacrosse games 2:00	
	Lars Soccer Practice 6:00-7:00	Jill Dance class 6:15-7:30		6:00 Dad poker night			

Autumn Schedule

IN OUR FAST AND FURIOUS WAY, we are not going to rely overly much on preparations (remember that over-preparation can be a pitfall!) but some *modest quick* planning—for most people, twenty minutes or so—will make us more efficient. Efficiency also dictates that this step take place in the days *before* you tackle your project, so if you need to purchase something it can happen efficiently—*within* your regular shopping trip.

You may not need to do all of the prep work described here—perhaps you're already familiar with your local charities—but do glance over these preparatory tasks to see which apply to you. You want to get the mental (and emotional!) juices flowing, grappling with closure as you think about what to let go, cogitating quietly on space and functions, or brainstorming streamlined systems with family and friends. When the time comes, you'll work faster and more efficiently, with fewer surprises, and defined goals.

SCHEDULE YOUR PROJECT

One of the most common reasons people fail to get and stay organized is the failure to schedule *adequate* time. When we organize, things get worse before they get better. Tearing apart a room and then leaving it to deteriorate while you wait for a chance to get back to it is so destructively inefficient that it will leave you worse off than when you started. Organizing is always most *efficient* (and successful) if one room is completed, in one session, before moving on to another.

Take out your calendar and walk around your space. Go room by room, scheduling consecutive days for each "room project," respectively, always allowing for more time than you need. Finishing early, so that you have unexpected free time, is never a problem. An abandoned project with no time left to put things back in order will only drag you further into the pit of clutter.

> **Fast and Furious Tip:** If you have young children and both parents need to tackle the job, choose days when the children are at school or have an activity, or make "babysitter acquisition" part of the scheduling process.

TIPS FOR SCHEDULING FOR SUCCESS

- Always schedule consecutive days until the project is complete.

- Clear your calendar for the day after the project in case it runs over.

- Get support (such as from a spouse or friend) for large projects. Two people work more efficiently and make better decisions than one.

- Treat this like a full workday and get started by 9:30 a.m. Everyone is more efficient when they are fresh.

Below I have provided a template for an *average* home based on a six-to-eight-hour workday:

ROOM	SCHEDULE
Master bedroom	2 people for 8 hours across 2 consecutive days
Bathroom/toiletries	1 person for 4 hours, 1 day
Basement	2 people for 15 hours across 3 consecutive days
Garage	2 people for 12 hours across 3 consecutive days
Living room/family room (not toys)	1 person for 2 hours, 1 day
Play room	2 people for 6 hours across 2 consecutive days
Children's bedroom	2 people for 6 hours across 2 consecutive days
Office/paperwork	2 people for 24 hours across 5 consecutive days
Kitchen	2 people for 8 hours across 2 consecutive days

What does this template tell you? It should tell you that even a large, very cluttered home can be organized in two to three weeks. If you work fast and furiously, your life can change between full moons. What other major life changes can you accomplish so quickly? I defy you to grow a baby, lose twenty pounds, build up a retirement fund, or get in shape inside a few weeks. Spread out and scheduled for one weekend per month, even a ten-room home will get organized between Christmases!

RESEARCH CHARITIES

Research your local charities by asking for recommendations from friends and neighbors, getting on the Internet, or calling the town clerk. You are looking for a single *convenient* local charity that accepts *almost every type of donation*, preferably in a location you drive by often. Your no-fuss reorganization project will get bogged down if all the stuff you've targeted for removal is still in the house at the end of the project, waiting to be placed on eBay, sold in a yard sale, trekked to a series of far-flung specialty charities or consignment stores, itemized for donation, or set aside to be sent to your sister who lives in another state. Fast and furious efficiency means that we want to get rid of every thing we've weeded—from toys to clothes to housewares—in *one* quick, convenient stop.

> **Fast and Furious Tip:** If you have a lot of family heirlooms that you aren't using, email your family members. Give them the date of your project and a due date by which they must make arrangements and pay for shipping for any desired piece that you're releasing. Caution them that if no arrangements are made and the item goes off to charity, they must forever hold their peace.

SIMPLIFY THE RUBBISH REMOVAL SYSTEM

Simplifying the rubbish removal system is the first thing I do in more than half the homes I enter, and often 30 percent of the clutter is eliminated just by collecting and taking out the garbage! Why doesn't the client take out their garbage? Almost always it's because the garbage removal system in the home is either too tedious or complex.

In the home of one recent client, the outdoor cans were stored on the far side of the house—convenient to the curb, but far from the kitchen where most of the garbage was generated. By relocating the outdoor cans next to the kitchen door, we valued the efficiency of taking out the *daily* garbage over that of taking out the *weekly* garbage, and lo and behold, multiple smelly garbage bags no longer clutter the family's kitchen and halls. Simplify your rubbish systems forever by clearing the area and making it easier to access or by placing the cans in more convenient locations. If necessary, purchase adequate (larger) garbage containers, larger liner bags, larger sturdy recycling bins (they take longer to fill than paper bags), and a box cutter to store in the garbage area. Commit to breaking down boxes *as they come in* to keep the recycling area clear. You can store larger boxes flattened between the bins and the wall.

Before the day of your project, make sure you have on hand a *large* box each of two (to three) varieties of drawstring garbage bags. Varying the colors will keep you from mixing up the garbage from the donations. You need an economy size box of:

- *Large* black drawstring bags for garbage
- Tall *white* kitchen garbage drawstring bags for donations
- Construction-weight bags (if you are working on a large project like a garage or basement)

GARBAGE REMOVAL IS INEFFICIENT WHEN:

- It needs to be taken out constantly because cans or liner bags are too small.

- Outside bins are in a remote, inconvenient location.

- Paper recycling is tedious to manipulate into quickly filled paper bags.

- Bins are too small to accommodate bulky cardboard boxes.

- Adequate space has not been allocated to the garbage/recycling station.

RESEARCH CONTAINERIZATION OPTIONS

Research where you can buy—but *do not yet buy*—the items found in Step Five, Containerize. This can be as simple as popping down the home organization aisle of your local hardware or department store during a regularly scheduled errand.

For those of you who are familiar with local charities and the container sections of local department stores and who have a working rubbish removal system and plenty of bags on hand, five minutes of scheduling will be the *only part* of Step One that you will need to do.

WEED AND SORT

Before

WEEDING and the attendant act of *sorting* are the hammer and nails in the toolbox of any organizational project. As we sort, we weed out the unwanted. We will discuss later some of the reasons you might have trouble deciding what to weed and how much, but for now, let's just talk about the mechanics of weeding and sorting.

WEEDING AND SORTING IN ACTION

Let's look closely at how you might attack an individual space. For example, if you were working on the bureau top, you begin by addressing *every item* on that bureau top, sorting them into the following categories:

1. *Unwanted items* get weeded into garbage and donation bags. If you fill multiple bags that are in the way, make some quick trips to ferry garbage to the curb and donations to the front seat of the car. Go back and begin new bags.

2. *"Keeper" items that don't belong* in this room get sorted into "other areas" piles (essentially weeding them from the room). Dirty dishes go into a "goes to the kitchen" pile; a bicycle helmet goes into a "goes to the garage" pile. If the piles get too big and are in the way, remove them to the areas where they belong. Then go back and start new "other areas" piles.

3. *"Keeper" items that belong* in this room get sorted into piles by type, such as a "sweaters" pile or a "jewelry" pile so you can see how much you own in each category.

As you weed, address *every* item. Even if you think you're keeping every t-shirt, put your hand on each one and ask yourself, "keep or go?" Inevitably you'll find, hidden amongst the keepers, the mistakenly acquired, the too small, the too stained, and the borrowed and never returned ("goes to the car" pile).

Once the bureau top is completed, and if all other surfaces have been addressed, move on to weeding and sorting the contents of the bureau drawers.

These are the mechanics of weeding. Applied correctly, they often account for as much as 80 percent of the success of any organizational project.

WEED AND SORT PROJECT BY PROJECT WITHIN EACH ROOM AS FOLLOWS:

1. If the floor is cluttered, start there. A clear floor makes it efficient to move around.

2. Next, weed and sort surfaces—beds, bureau tops, and counters— so you have a clear area to efficiently stage your piles.

3. Finally, attack the interior spaces—drawers, cabinets, and closets.

Fast and Furious Tip: Give every possession a home, but don't re-invent the wheel. When sorting items into "other areas" piles, let the retail world be your guide. Staplers? They go to the office because you would find it in an office supply store. Light bulbs? They go to a utility closet or basement utility area as they would be found in the hardware store.

BEYOND MISCELLANEOUS: HOW TO SORT THOSE "I DON'T KNOW" ITEMS

Clients think that as a professional organizer, I am going to set up a revolutionary new storage system that will take care of all their organizational needs. In truth, I earn most of my pay during the weeding and sorting step as I help clients process what they will keep and, if it is retained, *where* they will keep it. Often, clients will stare in befuddlement at some homeless doo-dad that has been floating around the house for years, completely flummoxed by the need to sort the item into an appropriate "goes to" pile. They might even ask, "Is there a miscellaneous pile?" The answer is no. Every item has a named home, and while you can set aside an item in a TBD (to be decided) pile while you take a few minutes to process, the items in that pile must go to a permanent named home before the project is over. Here are some questions to ask yourself to determine where that home might be:

- To whom does this item belong?
- Where is this item used most often?
- Where would I find this item in a department store?
- How can this item be most easily accessed and put away?

WEEDING PITFALLS

Why do so many people have trouble with weeding? Let's look at some of the common weeding pitfalls and how to avoid them.

Weeding Pitfall #1: Holding on to Things You *Might* Use/Need One Day

Recently I stood in the eight-room home of a client—four rooms of which could not be entered due to clutter—as she recounted the "horrific" tale of the time she got rid of something *only to discover six months later that she needed it and had to purchase one anew!* While she berated herself for a minor $12.99 mistake in over-culling, she was blind to the vastly more numerous and ruinous instances of mistakenly keeping all those things for which she had no need. Yet it was the latter mistake that was sabotaging her quality of life! You can pretty much always reacquire a needed item, or find a comfortable way to live without it. But there's no comfort to be found in a house that is stacked to the rafters with "just in case" clutter.

The secret to an organized home lies in a healthy, but not flawless, balance of retaining and disposing. If you walk that line of keeping only what you imminently plan to use and getting rid of all the rest, you will sometimes make the error of throwing out something you later need, or keeping something that you didn't need after all. None of us is perfect; we will all occasionally guess wrong, but if we guess wrong in both directions about equally, then an uncluttered home is the result. In fact, to achieve organizational success, you *should* have gotten rid of one or two things you later needed to reacquire!

Other people come from long-standing family cultures of handiness and frugality. These values—so important in a bygone age when procuring goods might have required a ten-mile wagon ride over rough terrain—are not just archaic in our modern age, they may in fact be downright destructive. An uncluttered home requires that we own only those things we will use imminently, and that we avoid storing the rest.

If it isn't handy now, or imminently—within one year for things you already own, within *one week* for things you plan to purchase—then get rid of it or don't buy it.

Weeding Pitfall #2: Keeping Things You Don't Use Because They Are Unused, New, or Expensive

A reluctance to donate an item to charity because it has never been used, still has tags, or cost a mint can sabotage your attempt to de-clutter. You've already spent the money, now this object is costing you time, space, and *agita*. You wouldn't let your mother-in-law visit for even three days if she constantly pointed out your errors; don't let an inanimate object nag you that it is a mistaken purchase while it rudely clutters your space. Transform it from irritating failure to generous impulse by donating it forthwith.

Weeding Pitfall #3: Keeping Things You Don't Use Because They Were Gifts

Are you concerned that disposing of an unwanted gift is insensitive? The truth is, discrete, no-fuss disposal of an unwanted gift is not just acceptable, it's desirable. In taking unwanted gifts to the nearest charity, you imbue them with noble purpose by letting them go to someone who needs them.

Our society has two rules surrounding gift giving, and as long as you follow them assiduously, you will keep your home uncluttered and never give nor receive offense. The rules are:

1. When you receive a gift, thank the giver.
2. Never inquire about a gift once you've given it.

It's the thought that counts. Learning to feign pleasure at an item, while finding true pleasure in the generous thought, is one of the most important social skills.

Those who inquire about their gift, ask that you give it back if you won't use it, demand to see it worn, or tell you where to display it are retaining control over an object while demanding that *you* house it! They haven't given you a gift; they've burdened you with an obligation! If you have family members who inquire after their gifts, either choose to have a frank talk about the protocols of gift giving or resign yourself to a series of white lies: "The cat knocked it over," or "I put it away until the kids are older."

Weeding Pitfall #4: Keeping Too Many Family Heirlooms and Mementos

We all own items that have been passed down through the family, sometimes through generations. Even everyday items can be transformed into valued mementos when a loved one passes. Of course, we should all keep some mementos of the dearly departed, but there is a balance. A house that is decorated to your mother's taste, that is in fact a living mausoleum to her aesthetic, doesn't honor her most cherished blessing—you.

How do you choose what should stay and what should go? Here are some loving, reasonable guidelines:

- For things you don't already own, if you love it, *have space for it*, and will *use* it, keep it.

- If you already own one but it improves on what you already have, then keep it, *but* you must get rid of yours instead.

- Keep three "useless" items strictly for sentimental purposes. *However*, each of these items should be no larger than a deck of cards.

Trust me, you are not betraying the dearly departed by donating their belongings, nor are you losing them again. Instead, you're honoring their blessed memory by honoring their loved one—you.

Weeding Pitfall #5: An Overabundance of "Space Hogs"

Some items, I call them "space hogs," don't store well, and often are limited to a single function. One recent client, a baking enthusiast, had purchased more than half a dozen very beautiful stemmed and domed cake plates for those occasions when she wanted to make multiple desserts, yet her kitchen was so crammed with decorative space hogs that she hadn't cooked in it for years. When I queried how many cake plates the average home needs, she conceded that two are probably enough. (You may have answered one.) In fact the answer is zero. No one *needs* a cake plate; a dinner plate will do the job. All of the space hogs pictured below came from a *single* kitchen. The cabinets of this same kitchen also contain a dinner plate and a simple medium-sized serving bowl that between them, and with a little resourcefulness, could easily perform the functions of everything seen here. If your space is limited, consider that space hogs should be the first to go.

These space hogs crowd storage areas and contribute to clutter; their numbers should be severely limited.

A NOTE ON COLLECTIBLES

While helping an elderly gentleman pack up his condo, I referred to his extensive collection of miniature metal, wood, ceramic, and plaster-of-Paris replica lighthouses as "tchotchkes" (a Yiddish word for trinket or knick-knack). The gentleman soon became aggravated and told me sharply to stop using this word as it didn't apply. As the younger Jew, I asked him, curiously, "what, then, does tchotchke mean?" After some reflection, he replied that it is something you *want* but don't *need*. Eventually, we settled on the more diplomatic word "statues" to describe his lighthouse collection, which I refrained from pointing out were in fact items he wanted but didn't need.

I have always been grateful to this gentleman for providing a perfect definition for the word "clutter." Clutter consists of stuff we *want* but don't *need*. And collections, like this man's lighthouses, are *by their very nature* clutter. Giving precedence to quality over quantity counterbalances this. A collection of three oil paintings is charming; a collection of 500 liquor bottles is clutter.

Collecting is mostly about the "joy of the hunt." If you are done collecting something, even if the market has declined, get rid of it. You got the value out of those Beanie Babies when they provided you with an amusing pastime. Now they are costing you in space, stress, and clutter, so get what you can for them, or better yet, donate them to a worthy cause.

Fast and Furious Tip: Don't look through your spouse's or children's weeded items to see what you can reclaim or how you can micro-manage where it goes. Giving family members sole control—and privacy—to weed their possessions is efficient, supportive, and polite.

REMOVE

SO MANY ORGANIZATIONAL PROJECTS STALL AT THIS STEP. Clients have identified the no-longer-wanted items but don't actually remove them from their homes. So after weeding, the next step is to physically *remove* garbage bags to outdoor garbage bins and bring donation bags to the car. In some cases, if the car and garbage cans are full, it may be necessary at this point to make several trips to the dump and donation centers.

> We need to clear out the unwanted before we can
> finish organizing our space.

We also remove "other areas" piles during this step. Of course, if you remove an item to a space that is already organized, it will be obvious where it belongs. In an organized garage, the bicycle helmet belongs on the athletic shelf or hanging from the handlebars of the bike. But if the garage is not yet organized, don't get distracted into another organizing project. For now, the bicycle helmet can be set haphazardly anywhere in the garage. If it is in the room where it belongs, then for now it is organized enough. When it is time to organize the garage, its final home will be addressed.

Once the original project space is empty, give it a quick cleaning. Swipe off bureau tops, drawers, and so on.

TOP THREE NO-FUSS METHODS FOR REMOVING STILL USABLE ITEMS

1. Drop off at charity boxes located in parking lots.

2. Bring to swap tables at the dump.

3. Place curbside with a large "Free" sign. (This is especially effective if you live on a busy street.)

REMOVAL PITFALLS

Let's look at some common pitfalls that can ambush you during this step of an organizational project.

Removal Pitfall #1: Letting an Object's Ultimate Fate Control You

Controlling an object's fate through all eternity by fussing about whether it ends up in the right home, at the right charity, saved for a family member who lives in another state, or correctly itemized on your taxes will keep you enslaved to your material possessions forever. The perfectionist desire to wring every penny out of every item by placing it in just the right consignment venue or holding that time-consuming yard sale is standing in the way of an organized life. Isn't finding a conveniently located charity that will take most anything a much nobler option? We achieve quick results by letting go of things in the easiest possible way. And nine times out of ten, dropping everything off at one charity is the swiftest, most efficient, no-fuss method.

> Let go of the perfectionist desire to place every item you own into the home of your choosing, and you'll let go of clutter forever.

Parking lot charity drop boxes may say "clothes," but check the smaller sticker on the front. Many also accept housewares, books, and toys. Fragile glassware can to go thrift shops, the swap table at the dump, or the curb with a "Free" sign.

Leaving items at the swap table and even in some donation bins means it might not go to charity. It may in fact be resold at thrift stores. So what? Fast and furious means we don't micro-manage where it goes; we just want it out of our lives. Besides, as long as some of it is reused by someone who needs it, we help the planet.

> **Fast and Furious Tip:** For very large still usable items that you can't manage to haul to a charity—or even curbside—be aware that some charities will pick up. Also the slightly less efficient method of using an Internet swap (such as Freecycle or craigslist) is always an option.

Removal Pitfall #2: Holding on to Gifts You Forgot to Give

Many clients have perpetually forgotten half-wrapped gifts lying about the house waiting for the next gifting event to come around—a complex, high-failure-rate system of memory and scheduling. Fast and furious organizing tells us that "even better" is the enemy of "good enough," so put those gifts in the car and drop them at your nearest charity. In the future, commit to buying presents the week before you plan to give them.

Of course, if one or two "giftees" live close by, and you have plans to see them *anyway* within the week, then efficiency is maintained if you take the present to the car (if you're visiting them) or leave it out and visible (if they're visiting you) and present it to the recipient with the truth: "I bought this for you some time ago, never managed to wrap it, but figured that late and imperfect is better than never."

Borrowed items should have gone to the "goes to the car" pile to ease their removal. If the borrowed item is in the car, you can plan your route along the owner's home while running your household errands. A plastic bag will ensure that items can be left on the doorstep, even in inclement weather. For items that need to be posted, either scrawl the address on a Post-it Note and attach it to the item, or, if there are many destinations, throw your address book in the car. You can buy boxes at the post office and address them there. Don't fuss about the cost of the box or including a note. Fast and furious means "get it done," *not* "do it perfectly."

Fast and Furious Tip: Buy gifts the week or two before you plan to give them, so that when the occasion arrives you remember that you already bought something and where you put it.

Removal Pitfall #3: Holding on to Things So That You Can Itemize Them for a Tax Deduction

Laboriously recording every donated item to see a small tax deduction will derail a no-fuss, results-oriented approach. Would it really be *so terrible* if the government, the institution that provides financial assistance and medical aid to the elderly, subsidizes housing for the indigent, and furnishes a free and public education for the young, got a little extra from you this year?

The twelfth-century Jewish sage Moses Maimonides, in his "ladder of charitable giving," ranked anonymous donation as the second highest form of charity. So here is your opportunity to organize your life fast and furiously *and* congratulate yourself on your altruism while you do it!

ORGANIZING YOUR HOME IS THE GREEN THING TO DO!

As we all become increasingly aware of our planet's dwindling resources, the need to reduce, reuse, and recycle becomes vital. The good news is that organizing your home supports this movement. How?

If you donate that redundant power tool, then someone who *does* need a power tool won't have to buy a new one. The economy might shift (from manufacturing to second-hand sales), but the planet will thrive.

When it comes to reduce, reuse, recycle, the most *effective* habit for green living is reduce. To be green, commit to buying only what you *imminently* plan to use. Planet Earth will thank you for it.

HANDLING FAMILY HEIRLOOMS

In Step One, you emailed family members to alert them that heirlooms might become available. In Step Two, you weeded those heirlooms that no longer made sense in your life. In Step Three, you must physically remove those heirlooms from your space. If your family members have not arranged for shipping them or picking them up, now is the time to honor all of your family members—both living and dead—by donating those heirlooms to charity or setting them by the curb with a "Free" sign. Every family's most important legacy is the living. You honor the memory of the departed by making sure that heirlooms go to a home where they will be both needed and used, rather than clutter the homes of the loved ones who remain.

Donating items to charity should be as frequent an errand as going to the drug store.

Use the skills you learned during Step Three, Remove, to help you keep your space uncluttered. In the future, items should leave your home at least as often as they enter and in the fastest, most efficient way possible. Don't set things aside in to-be-donated "when you get the chance" piles, or they will forever linger, cluttering your space. Donations go right to the front seat of the car, where they can spur you ("I have to get this crap out of the front seat!") into planning your route past a donation site.

Fast and Furious Tip: Don't donate glassware to charities that require that you bubble wrap it. It's just too time consuming. Instead, pile it in a box and move it prudently, but not gingerly, to the curbside, a local thrift store, or a swap table where you can leave it as is. And don't worry overmuch about breakage in transport. You didn't want this stuff anyway. Just be sure to leave the box open so that others will see that there is glassware inside.

NAME TO CREATE BOUNDARIES

BREAKFAST FOODS

IN THIS STEP, you place items you have sorted into their permanent named homes. Naming the cleared space helps you create and define that home, sets *boundaries* for what goes where, establishes how much of any item you should own, and allows you to pick up any room fast and furiously once your organizing project is done.

In naming your space and creating boundaries, use a "where would a stranger find it?" model. For example, the boundary of your wardrobe is the size of your bedroom closet and bureaus, because, as any stranger might suppose, all of your clothes belong in your bedroom—not in the guest room, in your son's closet, or in the attic. The boundary of how many dishes you own is the number that will fit in your cabinets without juggling or fussing so even a stranger could help you empty the dishwasher. By placing items in the rooms in which they are used, and by limiting them to the number that will reasonably fit in that space, your home becomes efficient.

Once you've named the space, only eponymous items go within. So, the "sweater" drawer contains only sweaters. Still, within these guidelines, there is room to personalize. You may decide to choose a larger drawer for sweaters, or you may choose to have two sweater drawers. Just remember, keeping more of one category will affect how much of another category you can retain.

In some instances, you may have to go beyond merely naming an area and actually use labels. Avoid fussy label makers. A felt-tipped pen is a fast and furious get-it-done method for labeling.

After all of your possessions are returned to their named spaces, if everything fits comfortably, you're done! No need to go on to Step Five, Containerize! However, if your stuff doesn't fit comfortably, or if there is overflow, you have two possible solutions:

1. If you have the space for more storage or need specialized storage, move on to Step Five, Containerize. For instance, if you name your bureau top "jewelry storage" but all of your weeded jewelry doesn't fit into your jewelry box, you may be able to solve the problem by buying a second jewelry box for the bureau top or placing some adhesive hooks from which to hang necklaces on the walls above the bureau.

2. However, if there is no room for more storage, you will have to return to Step Two and do some more weeding. I call this second weeding "the brutal second purge" because this is the stuff you *want* to keep but just don't have room for. This is the moment when to achieve success, you have to obey the Golden Rule of Organizing.

THE GOLDEN RULE OF ORGANIZING: INVENTORY MUST CONFORM TO STORAGE

As a professional organizer, I have many weapons in the battle against clutter. One of the most powerful is the strict and immediate adherence to the rule that *inventory must conform to storage*. It is, in fact, the basis for Step Four, Name to Create Boundaries. So, if you own a ten-room home, the boundary of your possessions is ten rooms, not eleven. If you're backpacking around Europe, the boundary of your possessions is a backpack, not a backpack and one floor lamp. Because even though you might be able to physically haul around that floor lamp, this boundary buster will be a constant hassle as you struggle to stow it under too-small seats, bang it through crowded doorways, and trip over it in tiny train restrooms.

What does this mean as you return items to their named spaces in your home? It does *not* mean *filling* your storage space so that you're committed to playing a Rubik's Cube jigsaw of shuffling and rearranging every time you need something. Nor does it mean renaming remote areas to handle the overflow. Efficiency is maintained when we store things where we use them. Maybe you can manage rifling through overcrowded cabinets or running to the basement for oversized casseroles, but is that efficient?

Inventory conforms to storage when a space is *empty enough* and convenient enough that everything in it is *easy to access and easy to put away.*

ORGANIZING PRINCIPLE: SPACE IS YOUR MOST PRECIOUS POSSESSION

The organizational precept that my gourmet client from chapter 1—and so many modern families—are just beginning to learn is that *space is your most precious possession.* If you can't sit on the couch, eat at the table, cook in the kitchen, invite a guest into the guest room, or park your car in the garage, then you have sacrificed your space to store stuff. The irony is that now you no longer have the space to use all of this stuff.

Let's look at some of the areas where so many people get hung up valuing stuff over space and how reasonable boundaries can launch us off the shoals of clutter.

Boundary-Setting Pitfall #1: Memorabilia Overload

We all have memorabilia—a high school yearbook, a wedding dress—but if our homes become a monument to sentimentality, a museum devoted to every camp t-shirt and every athletic ribbon, then no space is left for the present. In addressing your memorabilia, begin by figuring out which pieces can be practical. For example, trophies make excellent doorstops, and a horseback riding ribbon tied to a suitcase helps with identification at the airport. Use your creativity, and you might find uses for more of your memorabilia than you think. When it gets banged up, frayed, or destroyed, so much the better. You got to enjoy and use that memorabilia and then retire it gracefully from your life to make room for new possessions and experiences.

> Anything more than one chest of memorabilia becomes a millstone around our present, and to others it can seem just slightly creepily self-absorbed.

As for those pieces of memorabilia for which there is no practical use, it's fine to keep a few as long as there is a reasonable boundary. A small chest, the size of a small microwave, like the one shown in the photo below, is a no-fuss solution for "non-practical" memorabilia.

Memorabilia confined to a small chest is charming. When it exceeds this boundary, sentimental items morph into clutter.

Boundary-Setting Pitfall #2: Over-Curating Kids' Artwork/ Schoolwork

Throw out most of the artwork, saving only a few select pieces for the fridge. After all, how much of your old schoolwork do you presently own and how much of it do you miss?

If your child is especially sensitive, designate a large drawer or bin somewhere convenient and gather artwork there as a way station. When the drawer or bin gets full, throw out the now-forgotten bottom half.

A single album displaying the best of your child's artwork and "journaling" from infant to graduate is charming; four boxes can be pathological for parent *and* child.

Three or four times *a year*, something will seem really special. If it is on an 8.5 × 11-inch piece of paper, so it's easy to store, then scrawl the year and the child's name on it and put it in a "keeper" art box. Oddly shaped art projects get used or displayed for a short time and then are discretely thrown out, no matter how special they are.

The plate in this "keeper" art box violates the boundary of 8.5" x 11" paper. It should come out to be displayed and then either get used (under a plant?) or tossed.

Fast and Furious Tip: Avoid scanning your children's art or taking digital photos of it. You're just trading paper clutter for time clutter. If you keep only four special pieces a year, you'll have a nice representation of your child's art that can be contained compactly in a single box or album.

In terms of schoolwork, the report on Argentina, even if it received an A, gets thrown out after a few days on the fridge, but any autobiographical essays (e.g., "What I did last summer," "What I want to be when I grow up") get thrown in the box with the keeper artwork for possible future inclusion in *one* album like the one shown below.

> **Even Michelangelo's mother couldn't possibly have kept every random, youthful scrawl of stick figure floating next to spiky sun.**

As for any backlog, get rid of the oversized stuff and throw the rest of it in a bin in the basement to sort through when you do the art album, perhaps after the child is grown. Putting off a few unnecessary projects until a more leisurely year, as long as the pieces are stored together, is the fast, no-fuss path to being organized *enough*.

Here again we have used some boundaries: the *best* of the 8.5 × 11-inch artwork, and the *auto-biographical* content that gives us a snapshot of your child. Years from now in a single afternoon, you can cull this *one* box of materials to create *one* photo album of your child's art and writings.

Creating this 36-page album, representing one year per every two pages, is a project that can be left for when the child goes off to college.

Boundary-Setting Pitfall #3: Micromanaging the Photos

I rarely go into a house where the client doesn't have an "organize the photos" project on the agenda. The tedious task of sorting pictures into groups, laboriously affixing them into an album, or labeling them in files on the computer is often a monumental one. Honestly, who has the time?

A no-fuss, efficient solution for managing the boundaries of your photos is to throw all the incoming paper pictures in a box; you need not label it any more precisely than "2011-__." When the box is full, write in the end date and start a new box. (One larger box for oversized pictures might be needed.) Some memorabilia type papers—the program for the dance recital, the newspaper clipping of your child's winning goal—can go in with the oversized pictures.

As for that backlog of paper pictures that you have laying around and that you've never gotten around to organizing or dating, for now put them in a few beautiful boxes (something like a hat box) and don't worry about labels. You can occasionally set the box on the coffee table for friends and family to look through.

EVEN SENTIMENT NEEDS BOUNDARIES

In the film *Bedazzled*, the main character, Elliot, played by Brendan Fraser, makes a Faustian deal with the devil to obtain the woman of his dreams. Along with proving the inadvisability of partnering with the devil, the film did a fair job of illustrating the boundaries of sentiment. When our hero's lady-love expresses a desire for a man of boundless sensitivity and deep emotions, Elliot wishes to be transformed into this paragon of sentimentality, rendering him insufferable. A person who weeps copiously at sunsets, spouts extemporaneous verse, and fawns over dolphins is, well, cloying.

The moral of the story is that even a noble emotion—sentimentality—without boundaries can be too much of a good thing.

What about Digital Photos?

Digital photos don't take up space, but they do hog time. If we wish to reclaim living our lives over documenting them, then we should simply stop taking so many pictures! Whether pictures are digital or paper, reduce your picture taking to ten pictures a year. Two should be enough of any child's birthday, one in front of the cake, and one with all of the guests, three from any trip, but always with people in them. Leave the shot of the Acropolis for a postcard. You just want a brief memento of your vacations, not a minute-by-minute travelogue. If this boundary—ten pictures a year—seems absolutely draconian, consider that if you take ten pictures a year and your child lives to be 80 years old, he or she will have 800 pictures! That should be more than enough to document a life, even for the most obsessive of biographers.

The method we use to organize our pictures, our children's keeper artwork, and our memorabilia is boundaries and limits (and a few pretty boxes). Anything more is too fussy for any family that battles clutter. When you retire, you will have time to micromanage the pictures and artwork if that is your desire.

Does all this sound disorganized or even irresponsible? Remember that this system is not about *perfect organization*, nor perfect documentation, it is about *fast and furious, no-fuss, sustainable organization*. It is about "organized enough."

Boundary-Setting Pitfall #4: Excess Craft and Hobby Materials

It is a fact universally acknowledged that a person of fine creative talents is always in want of organization. I cannot tell you how often I meet a "crafter" who no longer crafts because his or her inventory of craft supplies overwhelms any crafting space.

The boundary of your hobby is *available space*. If you break that boundary by owning more supplies or pursuing more hobbies than your space can accommodate, soon you won't have enough space to do *any* hobbies.

THE FOLLOWING ARE SOME COMMON-SENSE BOUNDARIES FOR CRAFTERS WITH LIMITED SPACE:

- Self-limit to crafts that don't take up much space—sketching, knitting, beading, etc.

- Reject overstock, retaining only those supplies currently in use. (For example, keep yarn only for the sweater *currently* under construction; toss or donate leftovers when the project is done.)

- Pursue crafts sequentially. (For example, be a weaver for three years, get rid of weaving inventory then pursue oil painting for three years, and so on.)

Boundary-Setting Pitfall #5: Bulk Shopping

Again and again, I go into homes overrun with crates of toilet paper, hundred-packs of office supplies, and cases of water bottles. The homeowners assure me that they are being both efficient and frugal by purchasing in bulk. The amount of capital and space they are sacrificing to store items they don't need now and may never need, and the time and effort it takes them to shelve and then retrieve these items from the remote boundary-busting storage areas (the basement) that can handle such large supplies, don't appear to factor into their skewed budgeting process. As for the "trips saved," these families are probably dropping by the grocery store once a week *anyway* to pick up eggs and milk.

Of course, there are always exceptions. For people who live in remote mountain passes and can only get to town once a year, and for my sister in-law who, while living next to the high school in Olathe, Kansas, fed four teenage sons weighing roughly 200 pounds (91 kg) each, and on any given night a legion (or so it seemed) of their athletic friends, a bulk purchase of 100 frozen burrito pockets made sense. It barely got her through to next week's grocery trip.

So if you are feeding teenage boys or waiting for The Pass to open, then by all means pay the membership fee, use the gas, spend the time, build the shelving, don your stock-boy apron, and expend the energy to store those warehouse purchases. For the rest of us, the largest pack of toilet paper readily available at our local grocer's, and that will fit comfortably under the sink in every bathroom (an eight to twelve pack) should see us through to the next regular grocery run, barring an unimaginable digestive disorder.

> Organization, efficiency, and frugality are preserved when we shop at our local grocers for the quantity that will see us through (barely) to the next grocery trip.

BOUNDARIES AND SHARING: DOS AND DON'TS

To get and stay organized, you must share the task of getting organized and share the chore of staying organized with every person who lives in your home. What you should avoid sharing, however, is space. One of the reasons organizational boundaries work is because *one person* is in charge of claiming and maintaining the space. If I were to share a desk with my daughter and husband, then every time I wanted to organize the desk, I would have to make an appointment for my daughter and husband to join me. Talk about inefficient!

Sometimes you have no choice. There are some areas in every home that *must* be shared. In my home, it's a shelf in the coat closet. In these areas, however, you can subdivide spaces to maintain boundaries. In our closet, each family member is assigned one bin to hold that person's hat, mittens, and scarf. This gives each of us a boundary for how much outerwear we can own, and it allows others to easily herd any strays back into the owner's corral.

CONTAINERIZE

CONTAINERIZATION IS ALWAYS THE LAST STEP. It is just not efficient to bring something into a crowded space before we've cleared it of clutter, and we don't know how much storage, and of what type, we will need until *after* we've weeded.

In my work, I find that a few styles of containers come in handy again and again. In this chapter, we'll review some of these versatile organizing tools, learning along the way that there is no need to get clever. Low-tech, no-fuss containers can do the job cheaply and efficiently. If you were hoping for a more glamorous, new-to-the-market, cutting-edge solution, consider that the "newer is better" edict is one handed down by the marketers and is a big reason why we are all drowning in clutter.

Readily available and relatively inexpensive "get it done now" containers can be easily and guiltlessly swapped out when your inventory changes. Your goal is not beautification, merely organization. Adding a no-fuss cheap set of plastic drawers in the closet doesn't prevent you from installing custom cabinetry down the road if that is your desire. But consider that if the volume and type of your inventory changes, custom mahogany cabinetry, which is not flexible and cannot be swapped out easily, may someday become an impediment to organization.

Fast and Furious Tip: Don't weed or toss out any containers you may already own until *all* of your organization projects are done. You may need them.

BINS AND BASKETS

A *clear* bin, depending on its size, is an efficient container for every category, from camping gear to Barbie dolls. Whenever possible, leave the lids off the bins or buy bins that have lids that hang from their sides, like the one shown below. (In dusty attics or basements where there is no moisture, rest the lid on top without snapping.) Keeping the bins lidless prevents you from making that fatal error—stacking. If you have to unstack a series of bins to get to a lower bin, then pry off a lid to put something away, re-lid, and restack the bins to complete the job…well!, could there be a more exhausting, inefficient system?

> Lidless bins allow you to put things away quickly and easily in one no-fuss step by merely "winging" things inside.

A *clear* bin allows you to see the contents without going through the extra fuss of labeling, or, when the volume and type of your possessions change, *relabeling*. In a living room, you may want a discrete number of lovely, cloth-lined rattan baskets for containerization. But understand that their very beauty and uniformity will impede your ability to know what belongs in which basket. In the working areas of your home—child's room, playroom, closets, basement, garage, laundry room, kitchen, and so on—efficiency should take precedence over beauty. Clear bins will keep you efficient and organized, and no-fuss organized spaces have a beauty all their own.

The lid on this style bin rests out of the way on the sides.

Open-front "stacking" baskets with low lids on one side, as shown in the photo below, provide ease of access. However, stacking baskets are *most* useful when they are not stacked at all! Placed on a shelf, side by side, they are perfect for everything from toy collections to toiletries. And in most cases they are open enough so labeling is unnecessary.

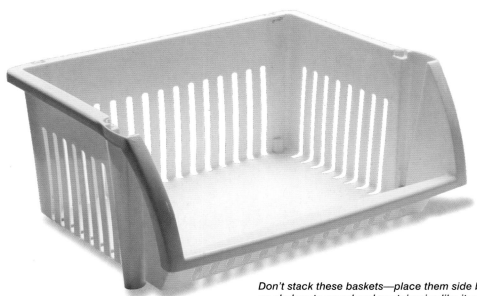

Don't stack these baskets—place them side by side on shelves to corral and containerize like items.

Fast and Furious Tip: When buying an open-front stacking basket, get a style with a closed bottom. Mesh bottoms allow smaller items to fall through. Also, styles that sport the low lip on the longer side provide the easiest access and more visibility.

HOOKS

Hooks like the ones shown in the photo below always have the advantage over hangers. It's so much easier to slip something on a hook rather than fussing with retrieving a hanger, "clothing" it, and then putting it away. The hanger does use space more efficiently, but fast and furious means efficiency of effort should *always* trump efficient use of space. For those few objects we wear and/or hang up most often—bathrobes, sweaters, "hoodies"—a hook will save effort. The clip-on-over-the-door hooks shown here are super efficient because they don't demand fussing with installation.

Place hooks in every bedroom, every bathroom, and near every door.

For your most oft used clothes and linens—bathrobes, cardigans and towels—these clip-on-over-the-door hooks are efficient to use and even more efficient to mount since no installation is required.

Fast and Furious Tip: For tight-fitting doors, buy single hooks and place them away from the hinge side of the door. Sometimes a door that is snug near the hinge will accommodate a hook farther away from it.

SHELVES

I have yet to find a family home that didn't need three of the resin modular shelves shown in the photo below in the garage and another three in the basement. Some homes need many more. Consider that scrapers, turtle wax, motor oil, jumper cables, windshield wiper fluids, and empty gas cans left on the floor create an unwieldy pile of clutter. These same items placed on shelves named "auto support" become an organized, easy-to-access resource for the homeowner.

This style utility shelf has myriad design advantages. It is tall, maximizing storage; it is light, so it can be moved by one person; it is sturdy, so it can hold heavy objects; and it is modular, so the height can be adjusted.

Shelving is an indispensible tool in the utility areas of an organized home. This modular shelf is both lightweight and sturdy.

Shelving is almost always the most efficient (though not necessarily the most beautiful) storage solution. Inside the home, prefabricated, finished, easy-to-assemble shelves like the one shown in the photo below can store toys, books, kitchen equipment, craft supplies, and clothing. A tall shelving unit gives maximum storage with minimum footprint.

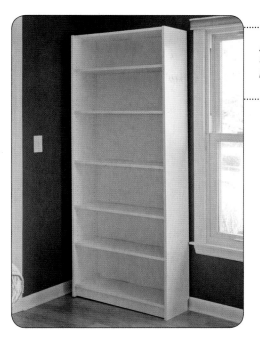

A tall finished shelving unit can provide maximum storage with minimum footprint and looks appropriate in almost any room.

SPECIALTY CONTAINERS

Because the containers in this chapter are simple and also versatile, they can be re-purposed as the volume and type of your inventory changes. But before we conclude our chapter, let's take a minute to talk about whether specialty containers are ever appropriate and how to decide which ones might be useful in your home.

Before purchasing *any* specialty storage container, ask yourself—is it *efficient*? How many steps does it take to put something away? Does it interfere with cleaning? Is it even providing a *needed* service or is it just marketing propaganda?

Does your china need a quilted dust cover when it is already stored in a closed cabinet? If you are living outside an earthquake zone, do your Christmas ornaments need expensive foamboard boxes with articulated bin-style inserts when they are only traveling as far as the basement? Just how efficient are those under-bed storage boxes if you have to remove them to vacuum?

Although we all indulge in one or two storage inefficiencies, they should be the exception rather than the rule. In deciding where and how to indulge yourself, keep the mantra of efficiency in mind. A single under-bed storage box, on wheels, with a center hinge in the lid (so the whole box needn't be removed to shove something inside), might not be too much of an impediment to vacuuming while providing appropriate storage for rarely used evening bags or seasonal purses. How we arrange the possessions in our space should eliminate work, not create it. Maintaining our space should take mere minutes a day.

Buyer Beware!

Be wary of containers that promise you more space, but only at the expense of time and effort. "Vacuum" space saver bags, multi-tiered hangers, nesting anything, and lidded bins stacked up one on top of another (rather than side by side on a shelf) all seduce you into sacrificing efficiency to extend storage. Yes, you can store more (encouraging overstock!), but it isn't worth the sacrifice of time, effort, and efficiency.

FIVE CONTAINERIZATION TIPS

1. Store items on the wall or on a shelf, *never* on the floor. Tools on the floor are dangerous clutter; tools on a shelf are easy to access and organized enough.

2. Go up, not out. Carve out more storage space by replacing short or low shelving units and bureaus with tall shelving units and tall bureaus.

3. Value the "rough storage" areas in your home, such as the basement or attic. Keep them accessible and install adequate lighting.

4. Don't continually build storage. Instead, reduce possessions.

5. Don't spend money on expensive custom closets until you have weeded your wardrobe. You may not need as much custom cabinetry as you think.

CHAPTER 2

HOW TO DEFEND YOUR HOME FROM CLUTTER FOREVER

WE'VE ALREADY LEARNED that to get our homes organized, we need to follow one of the golden rules of organizing: Inventory must conform to storage. But to *stay* organized, the boundaries we create must be *maintained*. It makes no sense to reduce our possessions to fit our space and then continue to purchase more possessions. Yet in this modern age, shopping is considered a form of *recreation*! And once an object is in our home, we shouldn't accept that we are bound to it in holy wedlock until death do us part. Let's look at some rules we must follow to defend our homes from clutter forever.

RULE #1: AVOID FREEBIES

In a former age, the whole family shared one bottle of shampoo and one tube of toothpaste. Now our bathrooms hold enough "product" to doll up the Rockettes. Never mind the advertisements and articles telling us how to achieve a perfect party (buy this stuff!), a romantic bedroom (buy this stuff!), an outdoor entertainment area (buy this stuff!), or an organized closet (buy this stuff!). We are promised that we will be cooler, hipper, happier, and more attractive if we just *buy this stuff*!

And if the stuff is "free" or a "good deal," we behave like ravenous wolves, greedily consuming without thought to the ruinous cost in time, effort, and space. We must realize that freebies and giveaways aren't gifts. Rather, *they* are the wolf, the enemy, the excess that gobbles our space and eats our time.

Top Five "Costly" Freebies

1. Buy one get one free (or get one half off) products
2. "Free gifts" given with a subscription/membership/attendance
3. Party favors
4. Giveaway (with logo) t-shirts/water bottles/caps/tote bags
5. Prizes

RULE #2: BUY ONLY WHAT YOU ABSOLUTELY NEED

To ensure that you make your purchase decisions wisely, remember that the boundary of an organized home should sync right up to your shopping list. *Nothing* should ever be purchased that hasn't lived for some period of time on a shopping list. It doesn't matter if it's on sale, if you'll get a second half off, or if it comes with a "free gift."

Whether it's groceries, clothes, or hardware, we must acquire only items for which an imminent need has *already* been identified and the shopping list assures us that it has. Out of milk? Put it on the list. The hardware store has a dazzling new power tool on sale that just might come in handy, but isn't on the list? Leave it. The conference is giving away free tote bags and water bottles? Leave them and run!

Don't fret that it might not be there later, that you might have to make an extra trip back to get it, or that it is easier to return it. In the long run, for the good of your wallet, the conservation of your time, and the de-cluttering of your home, you are always better off going back to get "it" *once you actually need it*. Of course, the marketers prefer that you buy now and think/plan later, shouting that it is good for the economy, but never whispering that it is disastrous for the planet—or for you.

When your home isn't crammed with unneeded items, it is more effortlessly maintained.

As for your fears, if you do, by chance, miss out on the opportunity to buy something, remind yourself that you are:

- Resourceful enough to find something just as good

- Resilient enough to shake off a momentary frustration

- Mature enough to live without

Ultimately when you only buy that which you imminently need, you shop quickly, saving time *and* money.

Fast and Furious Tip: Before purchasing something, calculate effort as part of the price. If assembly or specialized mounting is required, consider that the effort might make the item too costly.

THREE ACTIVITIES TO AVOID TO KEEP YOUR HOME CLUTTER-FREE

Paying more will help you own less and, paradoxically, help you to actually *spend less.* To avoid impulse purchases, swear off (or severely limit) the following "activities":

1. Window shopping

2. Going to garage/rummage sales

3. Perusing sales and clearance racks, unless the contents are *already* on your shopping list

In sum, don't impulse shop or shop for recreation. Don't buy something just because it's on sale or cheap. None of this is worth the sacrifice in time, space, effort, or money.

RULE #3: STOP BEING EVERYTHING TO EVERYBODY

In Charles Dickens's *Bleak House*, Mrs. Jellyby is a woman of boundless generosity and good works. She devotes hours to various committees and fundraises for the betterment of indigent Africans. While she is hard at work attempting to improve the lives of African children, her own large brood remains unwashed, unfed, and uneducated.

Let's look at a modern scenario. One recent client spent all of her time and energy volunteering at the Army base, but when her husband came home from his deployment overseas, the house was so cluttered, much of it with volunteer supplies, that most of the rooms were unusable. While this client was generously attempting to improve the lot of other Army families and the troops, the one soldier and family for whom she could do the most—her own—was neglected. Generosity is a wonderful trait, but when solicitude for others ambushes your family's comfort, remember that charity starts at home.

FIVE SIGNS OF OVER-COMMITMENT OR GENEROSITY TO A FAULT

1. Storing the belongings of extended family members and/or storing equipment belonging to an institution or organization

2. Picking up sale items to pass on to other family members

3. Insisting on bringing gifts whenever you visit a family with children

4. Exchanging holiday gifts with a too-large circle of colleagues and acquaintances

5. Volunteering continuously to the exclusion of family dinners, home maintenance, and family time

RULE #4: ELIMINATE TIME HOGS

"Time hogs" can disguise themselves as responsibility or even as fun. A recent client wanted to paint a trompe l'oeil mural in her hallway but never really had the time to complete the job. Another purchased specialty art objects that were too heavy or awkward for her—a non-handyman type—to hang. Even tasks that seem responsible can turn into time hogs. Here are a few examples:

- Coupons save pennies but can seduce us into spending more and tying up our money in overstock while costing us time, effort, and space.

- Craft projects that have lingered for months, waiting to be completed, promise fun while costing time and adding clutter and stress.

- Home improvement projects that require a large outlay of time for a minor aesthetic improvement that could be realized in a simpler, quicker way.

- Redundant systems—scanning pictures or transforming any hard copies into virtual copies—waste our time.

If a project or a responsibility has been on your plate or calendar, uncompleted or unperfected for months—get rid of it. It is clearly a time hog.

RULE #5: DEVOTE A FEW MINUTES A DAY TO FAST AND FURIOUS UPKEEP

Other organizing books will tell you that you can *get* organized in "five minutes a day." Such claims are patently false. However, it *is* absolutely possible to *stay* organized in just a few minutes a day. In fact, the *only* way to stay organized is to schedule several minutes of fast and furious pickup time *daily*.

If you store your limited possessions within boundaries, you should be able to pick up every room in your home in under three minutes. What does this mean in terms of scheduling? That depends on your lifestyle. When my kids were little, we did a quick cleanup every day before Daddy came home, so he could walk into a clean house. My husband and I did another quick cleanup before bed, so that we would both wake up to a clean house. These sessions—because they were done twice daily—took no more than five minutes each. For you, a single after-dinner or after-breakfast fast and furious cleanup may be more appropriate.

Some rooms regularly become very messy or require more than one person to maintain. In our home, it was the children's playroom; in your home, it might be the workshop. But as long as you indulge in extremely messy activities in only *one* room in your home, and so long as that room has a door, this longer pickup session can be put off to the weekend. Half an hour on Sunday evening with all three kids and two adults was more than adequate time to pick up our playroom. Neither undue hardship nor any great investment in time was required, even in this messiest room, because pickup was regularly scheduled.

Regular dishwashing is an efficient system that will improve your quality of life.

The exception to this three-minute rule is the kitchen, yet even a large meal, like dinner, if the kitchen is efficient, shouldn't require more than a ten-minute cleanup. But be warned: There is no kitchen that can maintain efficiency if the homeowner isn't committed to dishwashing after every meal. After all, those dishes have to be washed at some point *anyway*. Getting to them before the food has crusted over and before they clutter the sink and counters (rendering the workspace inefficient for prepping your next meal) will keep your home running smoothly. It's just more efficient to clean dirty dishes as they are created.

> **Fast and Furious Tip:** Schedule an extra two to ten minutes of cleanup time into every snack or meal. Your kitchen won't just stay (and smell!) cleaner, it will become a pleasure to cook there, you'll eat healthier, and overall you'll save time.

If we're going to get organized fast and furiously, we must break the bonds of our comfort zones and refuse to "Feed the Beast." This is the monster who screams complexity over simplicity, prepared over resourceful, false economy over effort. In part II, you'll see how we've tamed the beast in a variety of homes using our five-step no-fuss method all the while cracking the whip of efficiency. These homes may not have the same challenges as yours, but compromises of space and some indulgence in stuff is unavoidable in any organization project, so the issues we address here should help you learn how to face the particular challenges of your reorganization. As you read through how we transformed these spaces, you'll see how and where we avoid the pitfalls, use our tips and rules, and employ our five-step method to fast and furiously create efficient, no-fuss, organized homes.

PART 2

YOUR ROOM

"Our life is frittered away by detail... simplify, simplify"

—Henry David Thoreau

-BY-ROOM

GUIDE TO NO-FUSS
ORGANIZING FOR LIFE

We've reviewed our five-step method, we've challenged those pitfalls that can sabotage our home, and, most importantly, we've placed efficiency at the front lines of our organizing battles. Now let's see how we can use our results-oriented, fast and furious, no-fuss five-step method to organize your home.

In this part, we'll look at organizational projects undertaken in real homes. Because no two homes, and no two projects, are exactly the same, you'll learn how to apply our five-step method to a *variety* of common organizational challenges. These chapters will teach you to take the general and apply it to the specific. You'll learn how, in any individual project, one step (such as weeding and sorting) might be paramount while others (such as containerizing) might be skipped.

Although you'll be privy to the reorganization of several real homes, the ages, configurations, and other details of the families who live in these homes have been changed to protect their privacy. Furthermore, some of the more common challenges that I have found in so many homes were recreated here to illustrate solutions using this space. To these families, both pictured and described, and to all of my clients, I would like to say thank you for trusting me with your homes.

CHAPTER 3

THE MASTER BEDROOM AND CLOSET

Before

THE MASTER BEDROOM should be the private haven of our busy lives—the place where we go to relax and rest. But in so many modern homes, the master bedroom is not an oasis of peace. It is just another chaotic room trapping us in stress and discomfort.

In this Before photo, we see the master bedroom of an average modern home. Bathrobes, towels, pajamas, and a change of clothes are jumbled on the bed. A plastic bag, earmarked for donations, lives at the bottom of the bed waiting to be topped off. The bureau (not pictured) is covered in toys, an overabundance of photos, and piles of folded laundry that won't fit in a single bureau. To maintain their closet (not pictured) in a reasonable state of organization, this couple has littered the bureau top with excess clothes, and accommodated the rest in plastic tubs that are doing double duty as a bedside table. A rickety folding table has been drafted as a desk, and its surface is littered with paperwork that won't fit in the inadequate black plastic file box on the floor. Decorative pillows lay on the floor, which is where they pretty much always live, in my experience.

The room is not badly cluttered, but it is heading in the wrong direction, and if some steps aren't taken soon, all signs of organization and peace will recede beneath violated boundaries, inefficiencies, and perfectionism. In this chapter, we'll see how this family used a no-fuss, five-step approach to restore their oasis of peace.

After

THE MASTER BEDROOM

STEP ONE

This couple planned by scheduling two consecutive days when they could tackle the room together while arranging for a grandparent to babysit. In the days before the project, they checked out the "Organizing" section of the local department store and warehouse store during regular errands. They also bought two types of bags—white plastic bags for donations and sturdy large black plastic bags for garbage.

STEP TWO

We began by clearing and making the bed to give us a large clean "staging" surface. We then weeded and sorted the bureau top, progressing through the bureau drawers, bedside drawers, and bins. On the way, toys went into a "children's bedroom" pile on the floor, and most photographs went to a pile on the floor called "attic crawl space," where there is a box of extra framed photos awaiting their own organizational project. The desktop was cleared of all non-paper items, its photos joined the "attic crawl space" pile, the knick-knacks went into the donation bag, and some dishes went to the "kitchen" pile.

The largest category, clothing, was weeded for the no-longer-wanted, too small, and too stained and placed in garbage or donation bags as appropriate. "Keeper" clothing was sorted into piles on the bed by type and owner. We made it a goal to eliminate the inefficient stacking bins that had been drafted as a bedside table, so the out-of-season clothing they contained also got a thorough weeding.

STEP THREE

The large black garbage bag that had already been earmarked for donation had sabotaged the room for months while it waited to be filled and the contents inventoried for deduction—a removal pitfall we discussed earlier. This bag was removed to the car, along with the other bags of donations. To get the room done fast and furiously, the couple decided that they wouldn't slow the process to record minor tax deductions.

The toys were taken to the children's bedrooms, the dishes went to the kitchen, most pictures went to the attic crawl space, and one picture was hung on an available hook. Only two were left on the bureau top. Garbage went to the curb. The surfaces and inside of the bureau drawers were then given a quick swipe with a damp rag.

STEP FOUR

Although this room is named "bedroom," an office had invaded the space. The bedroom can't be a sanctuary if you have to face bill-paying every time you enter it. And wardrobe storage is compromised when office furniture takes the place of bureaus. This family happened to already have a perfectly spacious spare room set aside as an office, but an older computer and some drifting papers burst its boundaries into this room. After weeding, it became obvious that we were going to need extra storage for the couple's clothing, and that this boundary-busting office was going to have to go. For this family, going back and weeding the computers to one per adult allowed them to re-establish a bedroom boundary and consolidate papers in the office, which is well-equipped with the right tools to keep all paperwork in one place handy and easy to process.

Over-the-door hooks help keep clothes from becoming clutter on the bedroom floor.

> The office should never share space with an already hardworking area like a bedroom.

Once the office was removed from the bedroom, we addressed the clothes. All the couple's non-hanging clothes needed to fit within the boundary of the bureau drawers. As many clothes as would comfortably fit were returned to these newly named drawers ("his sock drawer," "her t-shirt drawer," etc.). The names give each type of inventory a permanent home and each spouse a boundary. If the t-shirt inventory grows beyond the boundary of the t-shirt drawer (that is, to a volume that makes it difficult to open or close the drawer), it will again be time to weed t-shirts.

STEP FIVE

The couple cast a quick eye over the variety of clothing that *still needed a home* and were advised to purchase, cheaply and quickly, at a thrift store or used-furniture store, a dark wood bedside table with at least three drawers and a dark-toned bureau to "containerize" their remaining clothes. While they were out, they dropped off the donations and picked up some over-the-door hooks for hanging the bathrobes, nightgowns, towels, and "hoodies" that formerly littered the bed.

Why hadn't this couple purchased a second bureau before this? Our old enemy perfectionism was again to blame. They could not yet afford to buy the matching piece to their attractive bedroom set, and so they waited, while their room played host to plastic tubs and clothing piles.

The Results and Our No-Fuss Solutions

In the After picture on page 69, we see a fast and furious, efficient, no-fuss reorganization. The new bureau is not as attractive as the owner's other pieces, but *any* bureau is more attractive than clothes piles and bins. A small bowl, corralling *one day's worth* of pocket change overnight, sits on its surface.

The owner's original bedside table has been placed on the more visible side of the bed, and the consignment-store bedside table is doing yeoman's duty, with its three invaluable drawers, on the far side where it can barely be seen. Although this couple is planning to eventually replace the bureau with their "dream piece," they are reconsidering giving up that hidden bedside table and its useful drawers. Practicality is winning over perfectionism.

WHAT IF YOU DON'T HAVE A SPARE ROOM FOR AN OFFICE?

For people who don't have a room to dedicate as an office, I still recommend, if possible, that the computer be kept out of the bedroom. If you have a living room and a family room, sacrifice the lesser-used living room to office space. If you have an eat-in kitchen, then consider turning the dining room into the office. If you have a small home and no children, then the office can be defined as a space within the living room. And even if you *must* use the bedroom, then dedicate a remote *defined* corner, and instead of rickety folding tables and awkward file boxes, procure the sturdy tools/furniture you need to create and support the functions of an office.

With weeding, the addition of a second bureau, and a practical bedside table with drawers, this couple was able to achieve the gold standard of efficiency. Both winter and summer clothes now fit in the bedroom, within the confines of their two bureaus, bedside table, and closet. Never again will they be prey to the unnecessary, tedious, and inefficient "seasonal switch." By weeding their inventory to *conform to the storage within the boundaries* of their room, by committing to "good enough," no-fuss storage in the form of sturdy second-hand furniture, and most of all by giving time and convenience precedence over stuff, this couple has created, fast and furiously, an organized, no-fuss bedroom.

If inefficiencies are the exception rather than the rule in a home, then the space will still be maintainable.

No home ever achieves total efficiency, but if inefficiencies are the exception rather than the rule, then the space will still be maintainable. So in this room, the flowers and photos—decorative and sentimental items, respectively, that do not add to the easy functioning of the room—were retained, but they have been reduced to a manageable and soothing number. Against my advice, the decorative pillows were also retained. A beautiful comforter and some lovely sheets and pillow cases would be functional, decorative enough, and less work—no need to throw them on the floor every night and pick them up every morning. But as long as this couple continues to indulge in *only one or two* minor inefficiencies, clutter will be conquered, and they will continue to enjoy a peaceful bedroom.

Fast and Furious Tip: Bedside tables should be large enough to provide adequate "bed support" storage for eyeglasses, tissues, lotion, and reading materials.

THE MASTER BEDROOM CLOSET

Typically, the greatest cause of clutter in a master bedroom consists of clothing piles. Let's look at another master bedroom that suffered from piles of clothing—in this case, the result of an over-stuffed and consequently unusable closet.

The large walk-in closet shown in the Before photo below is difficult to use. Indeed, it is difficult to enter. Still, some attempt at organization has been made. Boundaries were created with a "his" side and a "hers" side. His half of the upper shelf has another boundary, as it is clearly named "sweater shelf." The luggage is kept here (on the closet floor), adhering to the "keep it where you use it" rule, and two specialized tie racks (not visible in the photo) are meant to corral ties.

So why aren't the tie racks being used? And how did this couple, with such a large and lovely space, end up with a cluttered, inefficient, and stress-inducing closet? Most importantly, how do we get them back on track fast and furiously with our five-step method?

A quick rundown of the five steps will give us the general template of how we attacked this closet. But it is in the detailed review that follows where we will find some real-life challenges and their no-fuss solutions. We'll learn what drove our decisions, what compromises we made, and how we got the job done sufficiently, never perfectly.

Providing Access

For my petite client to keep her side of the closet organized, we had to create a system that allowed her to easily access the upper shelf, without having to inefficiently hunt through the house for a step ladder or chair. So, while we were out shopping, we picked up the sturdy stepstool shown here to use in this space.

A fold-away stepstool should "live" in every closet or storage area that has an out-of-reach upper shelf.

5 STEPS

THE MASTER BEDROOM CLOSET

STEP ONE

The couple researched the storage inventory of local department stores, put garbage bags (white and black for donations and garbage respectively) on their grocery list, and, most importantly, *scheduled one and a half days to tackle this closet together.* But life being what it is, when the scheduled day arrived, the husband was called away on business, so the wife had to reschedule several shorter, though still consecutive, sessions. This unforeseen bump in the road gives us an opportunity to see how we get it done anyway, without perfectionism or fuss, using some reasonable compromises. It also provides an opportunity to see the result if a vital step is compromised.

STEP TWO

My still in-residence client, the game if lonely wife, proceeded, with my help, to *sort* into piles everything in the closet and to set into "other areas" piles those things that didn't belong in the closet. However, we *weeded* only her side. This weeding was done thoroughly through all categories—clothes, shoes, and purses. In this way, the ill-fitting, the mistakenly acquired, the dated, and the stained were donated or thrown out.

STEP THREE

Next we *removed* "other areas" piles to their appropriate homes. These included some sentimental items that we moved to the "sentimental keepsake" chest in the guest room, some pictures that went to the "picture project" area in the front basement, and some posters that went to the "excess decorative items" shelf in the basement. Donation bags were taken down to the car, and the first load of garbage bags was removed to the outside rubbish bins. The floors were then given a quick vacuum and the shelves wiped.

By defining a permanent *named* home and placing objects within them— pictures to "picture project" area, unused decorative items to an "excess decorative items" shelf, and so on—we transform stressful clutter into organized possessions.

STEP FOUR

As we returned items to the closet, we *named* all of the spaces, creating boundaries. On the wife's side, our names and boundaries divided the upper shelf into a sweater section, a luggage area, a purse section, and a space for a *limited number* of special beaded or velvet shoes that would need a dust cover.

On the husband's side, because we couldn't weed without his input, the entire shelf was given over to sweaters. The clothing itself was returned by type and length. All hanging clothes were segregated by length to create space below the shorter items. Enough space was created to accommodate shoe racks under the hanging clothes. We were careful to maintain our sorting— placing all of his sweaters together, hanging all his blue shirts together, and so on—so he would know how much he owns in each "category."

STEP FIVE

With as many items returned as possible, the closet, though organized, wasn't maintainable or efficient. Our inventory still exceeded our storage, and because the existing storage did nothing to neatly corral items within their named boundaries, we needed to add some quick, cheap, no-fuss storage solutions. Because we had done our prep work, it was a simple matter to move to the next step, *containerize*, and buy, among other things, some inexpensive stacking baskets, better hangers, a limited number of clear plastic shoe boxes for dress shoes, and shoe racks for the rest.

The Results and Our No-Fuss Solutions

Having run through our five steps briefly, let's look closely at some of the decisions we made, some of the compromises we lived with, and some of the containers and tools we used.

Replacing Hangers

One of the greatest visual upgrades was created by replacing the hangers. In the photo shown below, you can see that hard-to-work-with wire hangers from the dry cleaners were propagating in this closet, and dozens of tangled empty hangers sabotaged the space.

Awkward wire hangers from the dry cleaners sabotage closet organization.

Metal hangers were replaced with notched felt-covered hangers, shown below, that accommodate just about everything. They are great for regular shirts, pants, spaghetti strap tops, slippery silk formal wear, and boat-necked shirts that otherwise slide off and land on the floor. Because their "heads" don't swivel, they don't have relations with their neighbors, and because they are relatively slender, they allow for a little extra inventory.

For skirt hangers, we used a style that places the clips as close to the head as possible—like the one shown in the photo below—giving us that extra few inches of visibility beneath the clothing. For pants, we choose a simple style with a stationary, non-swivel head.

These three hanger styles are simple and efficient. Avoid tiered hangers that seduce you into keeping too much by valuing efficient use of space over ease of use.

Fast and Furious Tip: Choose suit hangers without a metal bar to clip over pants. Clipping that bar is just another unnecessary and inefficient step.

Arranging Ties

Before our reorganization project, ties had been flung over the doorknob (see photo below left) and littered every surface of the room, while the bulk of them carpeted the closet floor. When we look at the previous tie storage system (see photo below right), is it any wonder that the tie-wearer avoided the awkward fine motor chore of laboriously hanging ties on these hard-to-use, single-dowel-per-tie—style racks?

Usually in organizing ties, I advise severe weeding. In most professions, they are an anachronism, but this gentleman still wore one every day. We couldn't even weed the "no-longer-wanted" nor dated because the owner wasn't there to make decisions. So what we needed was containerization that mirrored the ease of the doorknob but allowed for many ties to be stored together. I suggested installing two cheap towel bars on the door, as shown in the photo to the right. The ties could be thrown over the bar as easily as they were thrown over the doorknob, and the width of the bar would allow the tie wearer to see many ties at once. Hopefully, seeing his large collection of ties together, easily accessible, would encourage him to do a quick weeding at some later date.

Below: Human nature will lead anyone to throw their ties over the doorknob rather than fuss with these hard-to-use tie racks.

A towel bar provides an easy-to-use perch while keeping many ties visible at once.

In-Depth: His and Her Sides

As you can see in the After photo on page 86, the closet looks neat and organized. Note that enough space was created under the short hanging clothes to accommodate a four-tier shoe rack. This is not my favorite style shoe rack (shoes tend to fall down between the wire guides), but because it is expandable and stackable, it *is* versatile. The women's shoes face the wall to keep the "flats" from sliding off. As all of the men's dress shoes have slight heels, they face out for greater visibility.

Fast and Furious Tip: A bookcase-style shoe rack is the most versatile, efficient style. It accommodates shoes of all sizes, and it doesn't require manipulating shoes into a flaccid hanging pocket, onto individual prongs, or jammed into constrained cubbies. And your most-oft worn shoes can just be kicked off and toed underneath.

Before

My client weeded her side of the closet enough to fit the suitcase up out of the way off the floor. She has pared her dress shoes down to three beaded and velvet shoes that are hard to clean. They are in opaque bins, so no need to label, and stacking has been *minimized*, so every shoe is easily accessed and even easier to put away.

In your home, the names of the stacking baskets in the closet will conform to your possessions, habits, and interests.

If we look at a detailed Before photo of the shelf side of the closet (shown to the left), we see that sweaters, canvas bags, purses, and shoe boxes all comingled on the shelf in a disorderly scrum. As you can see in the After photo below, once we organized the closet, stacking baskets—named but *not* stacked—containerize sweaters, purses, and canvas bags, respectively.

After

As for the husband's side, as you can see in the Before Weeding photo below, it, too, looks neat and organized, but will it stay that way? Since this gentleman was not available to weed his clothes, they had to be tightly packed. His baskets don't sit one bin high, but instead are stacked, making it difficult to access and put away his sweaters. I predict that they will soon start to jumble and trail out of their containers.

Before Weeding

His *fifty plus* blue collared shirts are all neatly hung, but they are so tightly wedged in that it takes two arms, an elbow, and some shoulder strength to take one out or put one away. I am betting that he will continue to fling his shirts over the bed and bureaus rather than engage in a full-body wrestling match to hang them up. What would I suggest to whip his closet into shape? Incorporating only two simple changes will go a long way:

1. My client wears blue collared shirts almost every day, but as he has several shirts in other colors as well, I would recommend he keep only five and reduce the other colors commensurately.

2. As for sweaters, they are space hogs and should be kept to a minimum. Two or three (the number his wife ultimately kept) should be enough to see anyone through a winter.

But I've been doing this long enough to know that this particular client won't feel comfortable with such a thorough weeding. In the After Weeding photo below, we've illustrated what this closet would look like, and how easy it would be to access clothes, if we limited the blue shirts to a more generous twelve, the other colors commensurately, and the sweaters to those that will fit in one level of open-front bins. The inventory is still large, but at least it conforms to storage, making everything easy to take out and easy to put away.

After Weeding

CUT BACK ON DRY CLEANING: BETTER FOR YOU, BETTER FOR THE ENVIRONMENT

During the weeding process, special laundry care items should be the first to go. The constant effort it takes to service high-maintenance clothes is fine if you're the Duke of Marlborough with a laundress and valet at your service. But for busy working parents, every item of clothing that requires extra effort should be met with suspicion. One or two sweaters or pieces of formal wear heading off to the cleaners every six months is fine, but weekly trips should be avoided. Consider that if you engage in weekly dry-cleaning, you will be forced to put both a metal hanger recycling bin and a large waste basket in your closet to efficiently catch the dry cleaner detritus. These bins will have to be emptied and serviced—requiring even more effort. Is the sacrifice of time, space, and effort really worth it, especially when there are so many lovely permanent press fabrics on the market? Reducing your dry-cleaning frees up your time and space, and it saves you money and reduces the use of toxic chemicals.

Transforming the laundry systems in your home from labor-intensive to labor-saving will go a long way toward keeping your closets organized, while minimizing the piles of unfolded clean laundry on your beds and other surfaces. In the next chapter, we'll learn some no-fuss tricks for getting control of the wash.

CHAPTER 4

THE LAUNDRY AREA, BATHROOM, AND TOILETRY CLOSET

Before

IN THE NOT SO DISTANT PAST, most of the populace had one, or at most two, sets of clothing—their work clothes and their Sunday best. A fortunate few had many sets of clothing, which were cared for by their many servants. In our modern world, we all own more clothes than the wealthiest Regency debutante, yet we don't have the services of a lady's maid or laundress. What we've lost in domestics, we've gained in expectations. Every item is cleaned after a single use, and a variety of specialized detergents (delicate only, color-fast bleach, fabric softener) are *de rigueur*, or so the detergent companies tell us. These labor-intensive standards are complicating our bid for an organized life.

The laundry room shown in this Before photo has generous storage space, but it is so poorly organized that the detergent has no room on the voluminous shelving. The space that should hold the detergent is taken up by overstock/specialty detergents, a mixer, and cleaning supplies. Bulk paper goods are crammed onto the top of the cabinet where they can't be reached and are therefore never used. The rest of the cabinet is a mish-mash of utility items, excess towels and linens, toiletries, pet supplies, and lord knows what else. In this chapter, we'll look at how we can attack the laundry room, the bathroom, and toiletries. We'll start by looking at one family's laundry area and see how we used our five-step approach to getting it organized.

After

THE LAUNDRY AREA

STEP ONE

Planning this small job was relatively quick. We scheduled a single morning to organize the laundry room, relatively confident that two people could finish in that time. In fact, we did use an hour or so in the afternoon to buy some standardized laundry baskets and clear bins. Because the homeowners were already familiar with the organization sections of their local department stores and already had a variety of unused containers floating about the house, we didn't bother to scout the stores for containers. The job was small enough that we were able to use the family's household stock of plastic garbage bags—white for donations and sturdy large black for garbage.

STEP TWO

Much of the improvement in this room was achieved through weeding and sorting, followed by naming boundaries. As we look closely at what was weeded, why it was removed, and where it ended up, we'll see how weeding to conform to named boundaries transforms this space, and how it helps to make the rest of the house more efficient by placing things where we use them.

We weeded non-laundry room items by putting them in "other areas" piles. Toiletries went in a "toiletry closet" pile. Bathroom cleaning supplies were placed in a "under the bathroom sink" pile. Excess linens were weeded into donation bags or trash bags, depending on their condition. The mixer and some overstock paper goods went to the "kitchen" pile.

Categories that belonged in this room—pet supplies, light bulbs, and laundry support items—were weeded down to those items the family was *currently* using. Some items that were still "good" but that couldn't be donated because the packaging was disturbed were just tossed. Thus, candle-shaped light bulbs that fit a former light fixture were discarded, as was the ten-year-old leather cleaner that came with an expensive pair of shoes (long since gone) and the specialty upholstery cleaners that came with the couch and were never used. Because the laundry baskets were mismatched and unable to stack, they were condemned as space hogs and marked for donation.

The no-fuss method combats the perfectionist impulse to find a use or home for every obsolete possession—an impulse that keeps clutter in your home rather than in the garbage dump where it will ultimately end up anyway.

STEP THREE

The various "other areas" piles were moved to their new homes in a matter of minutes. The mixer didn't fit well in any of the kitchen cabinets, and so the family will have to decide if they have space to retain it once they do their already scheduled kitchen reorganization. The excess paper goods were stacked on top of the regular china to remind the family to use them within the next several days. Trash was taken to the curb, and donations were brought to the car.

With the "other areas" piles removed and the "keeper" items sorted into their own distinct categories, the empty cupboard was given a quick wipe down.

STEP FOUR

In the After photo on the previous page, you can see that the large *center* cabinets were identified as "laundry support," and only laundry items were returned to that space. The family kept a larger variety of detergents than I recommend, but because inventory conforms to storage, no organizational rules are violated.

Because the laundry support items did not begin to fill up the space, we drew a boundary and renamed the rest of the cabinetry "utility closet." By creating a boundary and naming the shelves, we avoid having this space devolve into a "catch-all" area. In the right-hand cabinet, the top two shelves were designated for light bulbs. Extension cords and adapters were transferred to a larger "electrical support" shelf in the basement. The small bottom shelf to the right was named "cleaning supplies" and holds just enough to give the major appliances in this room a quick swipe when they get dirty. The left-hand bank of shelves was renamed, from top to bottom, "batteries," "flashlights, and "pet support." This family experiences regular power outages, so having flashlights and batteries handy is prudent.

STEP FIVE

We containerized the space by doing the following:

- A small pink basket the family already owned was used to corral the iron and its unwieldy cord, making it easier to slide down from a high shelf.

- As shown below, clear bins (no labeling necessary) were purchased to contain the batteries and light bulbs on the top shelves so that items in the back can be easily accessed.

- A narrow garbage can (not pictured) was placed along the back wall to catch dirty cleaning supplies, lint, and clothes that are deemed too shabby to donate.

- An over-the-door clip-on hook, shown in the photo to the right, lifted the ironing board off the floor and out of the way without any need for installation.

- The laundry baskets were replaced with a set of matching baskets that will easily stack. Unfortunately, given space constraints, they must sit on top of the appliances, and when *all* of them are stacked up, their height blocks the cabinet doors, but unlike the disparate space hogs the family used previously, at least this neat stack can be moved in one simple motion.

Left: A clear bin corrals batteries that would otherwise roll to the back of a barely accessible shelf. Right: Storing items on walls or on shelves up off the floor reduces clutter. An over-the-door style hook eliminates the need for a time-consuming mounting project.

The Results and Our No-Fuss Solutions

To make doing the laundry itself more efficient, we also needed to attack the time hogs and perfectionist traps within the system.

Every bedroom was assigned a "hamper" in the style of a portable lidless basket. This makes it easy to toss clothing in, carry laundry to and from the laundry room, and dump laundry into the machine in one simple motion without the inefficient step of decanting. Adult baskets were taller, but for the children, we employed the same white open laundry baskets pictured in the photo on page 92.

Mixing colors with whites is a no-fuss solution that will cut down on both water and power usage and will not harm your clothes unduly, despite the protests of the soap companies.

Every family member was then assigned an individual wash day. For each child, a single load of mixed whites and coloreds took care of their week's laundry. Even the eight-year-old child was capable of schlepping her hamper down to the laundry room, running one load through, and then inexpertly folding her laundry and returning it to her drawer. This no-fuss system *eliminated* the tedious, time- and space-consuming "sort the family's clean laundry" chore.

As for towels and linens, they are not scheduled for a weekly wash; they are thrown in when someone actually notices that they are dirty or gritty. For maximum efficiency, sheets should be removed from the bed in the morning, and the same cleaned sheets should be returned to the bed that evening, eliminating the need to fold anything.

Fast and Furious Tip: Even if your system calls for a weekly laundry day in which all of the laundry gets done at once, avoid intermingling the laundry of people who don't share a bedroom. Each load should go directly from the dryer back into the room where it belongs without an inefficient side trip for separating and sorting.

SEVEN NO-FUSS TIPS FOR FREEING YOURSELF FROM INDENTURED SERVITUDE AS A LAUNDERER

1. Limit specialty care items (i.e. dry-cleaning, hang to dry, wool, lay flat-to-dry-clothes) to one or two formal pieces per family member.

2. Reduce ironing by buying only permanent press. For those few prone-to-wrinkle items, fold or hang them up still warm from the dryer.

3. Don't mix loads from different bedrooms.

4. Fold laundry in the room in which it belongs. Make the bed (roughly) before using it as a folding surface.

5. Never dump out clean laundry, fouling your folding surface. Remove piece by piece and fold. Bedtime will prompt you to put away any lingering piles of folded laundry.

6. Start by washing sheets first so that those same sheets can be put back on the bed that day.

7. Buy twenty-four sets of socks in a medium weight and in your *two* most often used colors. Throw out or donate all your other socks, forever eliminating sorting matching, and rolling chores. Do the same for every family member.

THE BATHROOM

Some while ago, I was hired by a middle-aged couple, recent empty nesters, to help organize their new "downsized" home. Because there was no master bath, the couple enlisted my help in organizing the newly renovated family bathroom. The storage in this room consisted of a diminutive cabinet under the sink and a tiny shallow medicine cabinet above it—hardly adequate for the modern woman's needs, much less a couple's. When I pointed out that the bathroom in this modest, four-bedroom circa-1960 colonial was designed by the builder to service five people, the clients were taken aback. How did that family manage?

Well, of course, back in 1960, a family of five would share a single bottle of shampoo, a single bar of soap, and a single tube of toothpaste. To that inventory we might add razors, toothbrushes, and some modest first-aid supplies. It all fit because no one in 1960—outside of a Hollywood starlet—had the variety and number of "product" that even the least vain teenage boy has now. The no-fuss solution to organizing this bathroom was to challenge every "product,"—every lotion, gel, mousse, astringent, after-shave, cologne, base, powder, cover-up, conditioner, and so on—my clients owned.

We needed to ruthlessly apply Step Two, weeding and sorting, followed by some clever Step Five, containerization, to the tiny shower, medicine cabinet, and under-sink storage in this couple's newly renovated but still small space, to finally achieve a room that is both beautiful and usable. In this chapter we will review their shower reorganization as an example of how to attack micro-spaces, before moving on to discuss what to do when a space is just too tight.

FIVE TIPS FOR ORGANIZING YOUR TOILETRIES

1. Throw away anything that has expired as well as all still-good but not-to-your-taste beauty products.

2. Don't even open beauty product gift baskets. Donate them to the nearest nursing home where they may be needed.

3. Double up. Use brands that you can share with other family members.

4. Rather than buy additional products, adopt your grandmother's frugal resourcefulness. For instance, witch hazel can be used as an astringent, bug bite cure, hemorrhoid treatment, rash and skin irritant soother, and shaving cream.

5. A plastic mesh basket next to the sink will capture your daily use products and will allow you to sweep them aside in one efficient motion when it is time to clean the sink and countertop.

THE SHOWER

STEP ONE

As always, we scheduled a day when both homeowners would be present. Shower organization is usually part of a bigger reorganization project (i.e., a bathroom). In this home, the shower portion of the reorganization project on its own would hardly take a few hours—the time it would take to buy containerization. We researched some container options on the Internet ahead of time, but this project was small enough that we didn't worry about stocking up on white and black plastic garbage bags because what the couple had in their home was sufficient.

STEP TWO

The couple agreed to severely weed their "product" to a single brand of shampoo with conditioner and a single brand of body wash that doubles as shaving cream. Excess and novelty products, mismatched washcloths, pumices, and scrubbies were donated or tossed.

STEP THREE

We took out the trash and placed a bag of donation linens in the front seat of the car.

Fast and Furious Tip: When weeding a bathroom, toss even mostly full bottles of no-longer-wanted product. In the future, waste can be avoided by swearing off the acquisition of so many beauty products.

STEP FOUR

The two tiny built-in shower nooks were named "shower support," and only items that would be used in the shower were now allowed within this boundary. The floor of the shower was deemed "outside" the boundary.

STEP FIVE

A quick trip to the local department store, dropping off donations on the way, yielded no-fuss storage in the form of suction-cup hooks that hold razors and a washcloth, respectively. These hooks, shown below, come in a variety of styles and are versatile enough to respond to any family's unique storage needs.

Although their newly renovated shower had beautiful bones, it was hardly relaxing when this couple had to slide on the soap, kick aside the fallen bottles, and wrestle the razor onto a crowded shelf to stow it. By refusing to store items on the floor, by insisting that their inventory conform to their storage, and by adding some inexpensive, easy, no-fuss containers, this couple reclaimed their spa-like shower.

Suction-cup hooks are useful for hanging razors and washcloths in the shower, keeping them off the floor.

5 STEPS

THE TOILETRY CLOSET

Unless you live in a very modern home, it's likely that your bathroom doesn't accommodate your bathroom support storage needs. While it's relatively easy to weed the products we use in the shower, what do we do about those modern pharmaceutical, beauty, and hygiene products that we can't do without?

In the last home we solved our problem by repurposing the couple's linen closet, located directly outside the bathroom door, into a bathroom support closet. Let's see how we used this same strategy in a slightly more challenging setting—a home with both a small bathroom and two teenage daughters. In this family, the linen closet was already being used for some bathroom support. But to turn this closet from the cluttered jumble you see in the Before photo here to an efficient and easy-to-manage space, we needed to tweak and refine their system, using our five-step method.

STEP ONE

We began by scheduling a generous six-hour day when every teenage and adult family member was available. Because these products and this space supported the entire family, we needed to have everyone present. We double-checked to make sure the family had on hand a sufficient stock of white plastic bags for donations and sturdy large black plastic bags for garbage.

> **Fast and Furious Tip:** If your bathroom is too small to add adequate storage, consider purchasing a shelving unit or armoire to place along the wall *right outside* the bathroom as a storage unit for your bathroom support inventory.

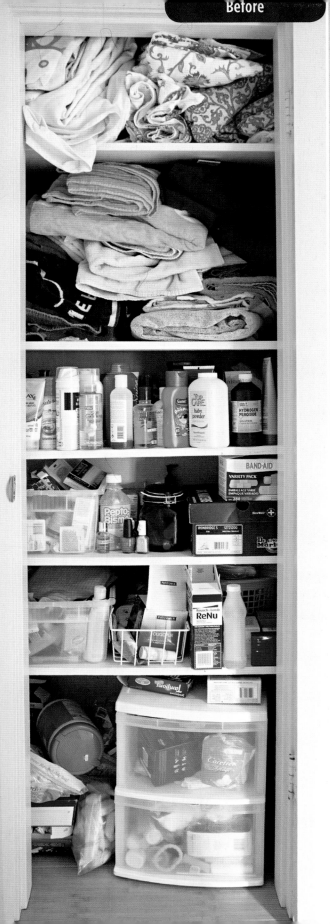

HAIR CARE

FIRST AID

HAIR APPLIANCES

SHOWER SUPPORT

TRAVEL SUPPORT

COLD/FLU

SKINCARE/SPF

NAIL CARE

STEP TWO

At the scheduled time, we weeded and sorted all the products from both the bathroom and in the closet. Expired products and medicines were discarded. Shampoos and lotions that had been rejected due to scent or irritants, even if they were new and almost full, were also tossed. Unopened novelty bath salts and gift-basket items were placed in a white plastic bag for donation. "Keeper" items were sorted into piles called "nail care," "cold and flu," "hair care," and so on. We used Post-it Notes to help us keep the piles straight.

STEP THREE

We removed the donated items to the car, and we took the trash to the outdoor trash receptacles. A large package of toilet paper was removed to the cabinet under the sink where it would be handy for anyone using the toilet. (Keep things where you use them.) Anything open and in frequent use (toothpaste, toothbrushes, some feminine hygiene products, one extra set of hand towels, and some washcloths) was given a valuable spot in the limited drawer space of the bathroom vanity.

STEP FOUR

There are a few areas in the home where I go beyond just naming and actually *label* the spaces. The toiletry closet is one of those areas. The size of the remaining inventory and the Post-it Notes gave us a guide in deciding on our named boundaries and how they would fit into this space. We could see that some categories would need to share a shelf, so containerization—to separate and then contain individual categories—would be necessary. The permanent labels would wait until we had our containers in place.

STEP FIVE

Open-front baskets and clear shoeboxes were either purchased or scrounged up from other areas of the house to give physical boundaries to our named inventory. Once containerization was procured, we affixed permanent labels. A good no-fuss solution is to quickly write the names directly on the bins with a felt-tipped pen, though some slippery surfaces require a sticker.

The Results and Our No-Fuss Solutions

In the After picture shown on page 101, you can see that this bathroom support closet now makes sense. Anyone, including a guest, should be able to both find and put away anything he or she might need quickly and efficiently. Let's take note of a few of the no-fuss details:

- A quick labeling—a felt-tip marker applied directly to the containers—was the easy, no-fuss solution for keeping this shared space organized.

- Because the family already had it, we employed the plastic drawer unit shown in the After photo. As the plastic is clear, we didn't need to label the drawers as "feminine hygiene" and "eye care." The products are distinctive enough to announce themselves.

- A clear bin is dubbed "nail care," while a basket is dubbed "skin care." The size and distribution of these categories in your house will of course respond to your individual lifestyle.

- Although stacking was not completely avoided, because the first-aid inventory was small and low, it isn't difficult to access in the lower basket on the second shelf from the top.

- Hair-care inventory was so large that a clear shoebox, corralling hair-care *appliances*, sits on the shelf next to a basket for hair-care *products*.

- Another clear bin has been given over to "travel support." Toiletry bags, already packed and ready to go, and some smaller travel-sized products are stored here.

Fast and Furious Tip: When organizing your toiletries, there is no need to re-invent the wheel. Group and name them exactly as you would find them in a drugstore: "skin care," "first aid," "eye and ear," etc.

When we look at why this closet now works, we realize that renaming the majority of it "bathroom/toiletry support" rather than "linens" provided a guideline for how much inventory and of what variety this family truly needed. The linens that remain in this closet—the family beach towels and a handful of guest towels—are rarely used and so have been relegated to a remote upper shelf. While guest towels fall under the rubric of "bathroom support," the beach towels (one per family member) could have been moved into the bureau drawers that contain each family member's bathing suit. But we'd cleared so much space, it just made sense to accommodate them here.

What happened to the rest of the family's bath towels and linens? Read these handy tips to see how we turned a linen explosion into an efficient no-fuss organizational system that can streamline your life.

THREE TIPS FOR LINENS

1. Reduce bath towel inventory to two per family member of a color that matches their respective bedrooms. Provide hooks in every bedroom; the clip-on over-the-door variety are simplest. This approach encourages children to hang up their towels after their bath, forever reducing laundry. Hold aside two sets of guest towels and donate all other towels.

2. Reduce sheets to one set that always remains on the bed and only one "backup" set per bed (for stomach flu days). The backup stays on the closet shelf in the room in which it belongs. Donate the remaining sheets and blankets.

3. A single comforter and a single blanket are sufficient for each bed. During the summer months, everyone's winter blanket should be stored on their bedroom closet shelf, in a chest at the foot of the bed, or in a blanket box under their bed. (Store things where you use them.)

In organizing the bathroom, toiletry closet, and laundry room, we used our five-step no-fuss method to get the job done—not perfectly, but quickly—and to set up a system in the utility areas of the home that is efficient and, consequently, maintainable. In the next chapter, we'll see how larger utility areas—closets, the basement, and the garage—can benefit from a no-fuss method.

Fast and Furious Tip: Do not push containers in your closets all the way to the side so that they are partially obscured by the door frame. It is worth the sacrifice of space to keep everything visible and easily retrievable.

CHAPTER 5

THE BASEMENT, GARAGE, AND UTILITY CLOSET

Before

AS YOU CAN SEE IN THIS BEFORE PHOTO, the basement in this home had become a dumping ground for all the goods the family was not yet ready to part with. Old furniture, toys, and athletic equipment littered the space. Furthermore, items that belonged in the garage—golf clubs and sleds—had eddied to the basement with the idea that they would be transferred to the garage when they were in season. Some leftover materials from recent renovations—including a couple of brand-new, expensive kitchen cabinet doors that were ordered in the wrong size—had also been stashed in the basement. This basement is further compromised by a defunct family business. The family-run accounting firm was closed down a couple of years before our reorganization, but in accordance with tax laws, much of the client paperwork, along with payroll records and so on, must be retained for several years.

So what went wrong in this space? How do we wade through this basement and create an efficient and organized area? In this chapter, we'll look at how to use the fast and furious five-step method to organize your basement as well as your garage and utility closet.

After

THE BASEMENT

STEP ONE

We began by scheduling two consecutive days when both adult members of the household could tackle the space. We also bought three types of bags—white plastic bags for donations, sturdy large black plastic bags for garbage, and construction-weight garbage bags for lumber and building supplies.

For large or labor-intensive jobs such as basements, garages, and paperwork, it's vital to schedule sufficient time and to enlist enough support.

STEP TWO

On the scheduled days, we moved on to weeding and sorting. In the course of weeding, it became clear that most of the toys in this basement were no longer appropriate for the ages of the children in the home, and, in fact, many of them had been placed in the basement years ago in preparation for a trip to a local charity, but once they had eddied out in the basement, they went so far off of the parents' radar that there they stayed.

The small round drop-leaf table on the right of the Before photo on the previous page was donated as the owner couldn't identify a need for it in the home. Another wooden outdoor table and its matching chairs, invisible beneath the pile of clutter, were taken to the backyard. The outdoor table was originally on the back porch until it was replaced by a nicer set. By placing it in the yard, rather than storing it indefinitely in the basement, we have reduced clutter while providing a garden seating area. Although the table and chairs will be exposed to harsh winters that will reduce them to kindling within a handful of years, it is better to have several years of use out of them than to leave them to mold and clutter up the basement, awaiting a "stain to winterize" project that will probably never get done.

Don't be afraid to use your possessions until they are used up or out. If they did yeoman's duty in our homes, we may all take comfort that they were not wasted before declining to a noble and dignified end.

Buried within the clutter, we found two bags of garbage. Because the family used the same bags for garbage, donations, and long-term storage, mix-ups were likely to occur. In our reorganization, we were careful to use different containers—white and black bags—to avoid inefficient double-checking or just this type of error.

Because their youngest child had graduated to snowboarding, the family decided to donate the sled. All other athletic and seasonal equipment was placed in a "garage" pile.

STEP THREE

After weeding and sorting, we took the garbage to the trash receptacles and removed the "other areas" piles to their new homes. One of the largest was the aforementioned "garage" pile. Athletic equipment that is regularly loaded in the car *belongs* in the garage. It is woefully inefficient to schlep outdoor seasonal decorations and equipment *through* the garage to go to the basement. By weeding these items sufficiently to store them where we use them, we've not only promoted efficiency, but we've *completely eliminated* the tedious and unnecessary "seasonal switch" chore.

Excess wooden trim from the kitchen and the wrongly sized kitchen cabinet doors, even though they were perfectly good pieces of lumber, were also discarded. The mistake of acquiring too much or the wrong item is only compounded by then holding onto these mistakes.

Once all of the "other areas" piles along with the garbage and donations were removed, we gave the basement a quick sweeping.

STEP FOUR

When we sorted our "keepers" into piles—"Christmas supplies," "household renovation materials," and so on—we had already really begun the naming process. The size of the keeper piles and the size and shape of the storage that remained helped to guide us into placing our named piles into spaces with appropriate boundaries. Some named groups were too large to fit within any of the remaining storage, so some containerization would be necessary.

STEP FIVE

As we worked, it became clear that we were going to need to do some containerizing or we would have to store most items on the floor, and after all of our hard work the dread "uni-pile" would be back.

In the course of the weeding, two long workbenches were revealed. Because the family was already using a third relatively well-organized workbench along the opposite wall, these two were extraneous. I recommended that we replace these workbenches with better storage, arguing that a five-tier utility work shelf would more than double the storage capacity of these two workbenches while taking up the same footprint.

A quick trip to the local hardware store (dropping off our donations on the way) yielded three clear tubs and three utility work shelves. A black metal shelving unit that had been cannibalized for our garage reorganization project (which you'll read about in the next section) was drafted for more storage.

The Results and Our No-Fuss Solutions

In the After photo on page 107, you can see a couple of the boundaries we created and how we used our containers. As you can see, despite my dire predictions, we ended up keeping the workbenches to use as wooden shelves. Although they don't provide as much vertical storage as the utility work shelves, the family weeded thoroughly enough to make do with the storage at hand.

In returning items, we "named" the various shelves. Under the wooden shelf at right in the After photo, we stored a discrete number of Christmas decorations. Because the containers are clear, they don't need labels. And because the family has pledged itself to Christmas activities (baking, caroling, visiting the downtown lights) and ephemeral Christmas decorations (live local trees, wreaths, and boughs and stringing popcorn and cranberries for decorations), all of the Christmas supplies fit in a few bins on the "Christmas" shelf.

On the same shelf, next to the Christmas decorations, we have a "household renovations" area. Replacement tiles and grouts for the bathrooms were placed on this shelf. Adjacent, standing between the wooden shelf and the utility shelf, is a box of ceiling panels.

Fast and Furious Tip: If you have earmarked something for donation, take it directly to your car! Usable items that are stashed in a remote location, "waiting" for a trip to the charitable drop-box, will linger, grow, and mutate into a mountain of clutter.

On the top tier of that same wooden shelf, above the "household renovations" area, we placed an "excess home décor" bin. These are the pictures, lamps, and decorative objects that don't currently fit in with the present décor, but that may get switched out or used in a future redecoration. When we define one bin, or one shelf, as the boundary for excess home décor, we create a reasonably sized area for those items that don't fit the current décor but that the homeowner loves and hopes to use again. As long as we have a reasonable boundary and a healthy limit (one bin! one shelf!) for these decorative items, they will not overwhelm and mutate into clutter.

The small black metal shelf on top of the left-hand workbench in the After photo makes up for some of the vertical storage we lost when the family decided to use the workbenches with their miserly two tiers. The top two shelves of this wire unit are named "Containerization;" they hold a small number of containers that may come in handy as our storage needs change. Again, as long as we define a reasonable boundary, a limited number of containers are appropriate.

The bottom tier of this black metal shelf is for interim storage. At the moment, it holds a small number of items that are earmarked for the oldest child's college dorm room in the fall.

We bought and filled three utility shelves (and the bottom of one work bench) with the accounting records from the family's former business, but we still have empty shelf space on the top of the workbenches. No reorganization can be termed a success if all storage space is filled.

There is one small boundary violation within this room. Can you see it in the After photo on page 107? A half dozen pieces of lumber were appropriately transferred to the true "work shop" area on the opposite side of the room, but one larger piece of plywood escaped our boundary. Due to its size and shape, it made sense to slide it behind the utility shelving where it would be easy to store and easy to access. You can see it under the light switch as a dark squared shape, the height of the lowest two shelves, peeking out at the left most edge of the picture. We left it peeking out so that it stays on the homeowner's radar. This is one of those instances where an odd shape or configuration compels us to store something outside of its boundary. But because it is a single item, and because we have kept it in the same room, we haven't sabotaged efficiency.

Fast and Furious Tip: Beware of filling your storage spaces with oversized cardboard boxes. Rely on your resourcefulness to obtain cardboard shipping boxes and gift boxes, in the dimensions you need, when you *imminently* need them.

HOW TO ORGANIZE A WORKBENCH AND TOOLS

1. Define an area as the workshop.

2. Procure a real workbench (every home needs one!), one to two utility shelves, and a case for small hardware. Choose a suitcase style that opens to show the contents of all its bins at once, *not* an inefficient unit with multiple small drawers.

3. Label the shelves like a hardware store would—"plumbing," "paint and painting supplies," "electrical," "door/furniture/window hardware," "hooks and adhesives," and "power tools."

Fast and Furious Tip: Guard your empty shelf space. It is a valuable tool, available for interim storage, when life's surprises happen along. A child suddenly moving back home, the death of an elderly relative, the dismantling of a summer home or family business all may require interim storage in your home.

Using our five-step method, we transformed this basement from an unusable pile of clutter into an efficient, no-fuss storage area. In our next section, we'll do the same with another large utility area that is all too often host to clutter: the garage.

TOP FIVE PHENOMENA THAT AMBUSH AN ORGANIZED BASEMENT

1. Christmas decorations. Don't turn your house into Santa's village. Limit yourself to three to four bins, and use the time you save decorating to bake cookies, go caroling, or visit the window displays with your family.

2. The seasonal switch. Weed your possessions down to store items *where you use them*. Out-of-season clothing and equipment stored in the basement will go off your radar screen and end up as clutter in your storage areas.

3. Inadequate lighting/ventilation/cleaning. If you aren't using your basement or attic storage because you aren't able to see, breathe, get rid of the dampness, or duck the cobwebs, consider restoring the space to make it welcoming. A well-lit, clean, dry space may double the footprint of your home and keep clutter out of your living areas.

4. Inadequate storage. Never store possessions on the floor. Sturdy tall shelves will make the most of your storage space.

5. Failure to schedule cleaning and weeding. Even a well-organized basement should get a thorough cleaning and weeding every two years. You'll be surprised at how many things you no longer need.

5 STEPS

THE GARAGE

Did you know that 25 percent of Americans with two-car garages can no longer fit their cars in that garage? In so many homes, the garage is no longer the space where the family houses primarily the car, with a little space set aside for gardening supplies and bicycles. Instead, it's the dumping ground for everything that should be in the house but no longer fits there. All of this junk is actually impeding the family's ability to access the things that legitimately belong in the garage.

Before

The garage in the Before photo here does not appear to be overcrowded, yet because items are randomly dumped, with no named boundaries or vertical storage, it becomes inefficient to find possessions and a true puzzle when one considers where to put them away. On our scheduled days, weeding out the old, the no longer wanted, and the mistakenly acquired was the first step in organizing this space in a sensible and efficient manner. But it was in defining and naming boundaries, and then procuring adequate containerization for what remained, that we turned this garage from dump to showcase. Let's do a quick review of the whole five-step process before we look at the particulars.

Fast and Furious Tip: If you live in an area with a tempestuous climate, schedule a backup session for your garage organization. A rain date on the calendar will keep your project from getting derailed by inclement weather.

After

STEP ONE

As usual, we started by scheduling a weekend when at least two family members could devote themselves to the task. Because we didn't have a third day, we determined to work at least eight hours on the first day, and as long as it might take on the second day. Knowing that we would need to buy containers before the stores closed our last night, we researched them ahead of time. The family purchased three types of garbage bags—white for donations, black for garbage, and construction weight for building materials.

STEP TWO

At the scheduled time, we used the sorting/weeding process to remove everything from the garage and arrange them in piles on the driveway dubbed "athletic equipment," "lawn and landscape care," and "automotive support." We also had "other areas" piles and bags for charitable donations and the dump.

STEP THREE

"Other areas" piles were taken to their appropriate locations. A quick trip to the municipal dump got rid of some larger garbage, and donations were dropped off on the way. It was necessary to do this step out of turn as the dump would be closed on our second work day. While the homeowners made the trip, I swept down the cobwebs from the walls and corners of the garage and quickly swept the floor.

Fast and Furious Tip: Call your town hall or your waste management services to learn what qualifies as hazardous waste and the dates and times when they can pick up, or you can drop off, these materials. Put the date on your calendar and gather the toxic waste in a single bin near the outdoor garbage area.

STEP FOUR

We determined which categories would go where and named those areas to create boundaries. The "keeper" items were returned to their named areas, but since there was no shelving, hooks, or appropriate containers yet, items had to be placed on the floor, and so the garage still looked cluttered. And because our boundaries lack physical expression, the room remained inefficient and unmaintainable.

STEP FIVE

Containerizing these items supported our boundaries and transformed this space into an efficient and easy-to-use storage area. The type, number, and style of our containers responded to the type and volume of inventory that remained after weeding. I recommended that we add two utility shelves and get a simple-to-install rack to hang tools from the walls.

The Results and Our No-Fuss Solutions

In our After photo of the entire garage, shown on page 117, you can see that we have created boundaries and procured the containers I recommended. We hung lighter items on the walls and used the shelves to store things up and off the floor, creating boundaries by naming our shelves and wall areas. Although larger items (such as the bikes) escaped our boundaries a bit because they needed to be placed where they could fit, they are easy to access and put away, so their "home" is efficient.

Now let's look in detail at some of the different areas of the garage.

Fast and Furious Tip: Most of us won't go to the trouble of lifting a heavy bike onto a hook or attaching pulleys to hoist it overhead. A permanent, convenient parking space on the floor is the most efficient system that will see our bikes easily *and consistently* stowed.

The Athletic Area

In the Before photo shown below you can see an overflowing garbage bin with bags of recycling leaning against it. Beach chairs, a skateboard, some lawn equipment, and rollerblades are all in a large scrum. To the other side of the door, old lumber, more garbage, and some fertilizer are tossed together in a haphazard pile.

We named this area the "Athletic" area, as shown in the After photo below. A new shelf near the door has been named "athletic equipment." Open-front bins corral rollerblades and frisbees respectively. A large clear bin on the second shelf holds an extensive collection of water guns. Instead of buying an expensive ball rack to containerize the different balls, we hunted around for a cheaper solution. The homeowner, in a moment of brilliance, suggested removing two of the shelves from a black metal shelving unit in the basement. These shelves sport a one-inch decorative trim that hangs down like a short skirt around their edge. When we turned them upside down (skirt side up) and placed them on the utility shelf, the decorative trim made a "lip" that keeps the balls from rolling off the shelf. (Think of the lid of a shoe box corralling ping-pong balls on a bookshelf.)

Before

A small black garbage can was drafted to hold hockey sticks and baseball bats. Along with the two bikes, it defines our "athletic" area. The scooters were weeded down to one favorite that finds a home between the garage doors. The manual for the alarm system, which had been tucked precariously behind the wall unit, was containerized in a clear dustcover (a plastic Ziplock-style bag!) and pinned to the wall next to the keypad. The skateboard ramp fits, upright, behind the scooter when it is not in use.

Fast and Furious Tip: Locate children's outdoor toys, bikes, and athletic equipment near the front of the garage. Children will rarely make the long trip to the back of the garage to put something away.

The Gardening/Landscape Support, Auto, and Beach Areas

On the back wall of the garage, shown in the Before photo below, more beach chairs, a dismantled and broken hockey net, an old foosball table on its way to being donated, a screen, some more lumber, more garbage bags, and some scooters made an undefined hill of clutter. Still, some attempt had been made at organizing. An old appliance box corralled yard tools, but the unreachable bottom held a graveyard of water pistols, balls, and garbage.

Fast and Furious Tip: In a wooden-framed garage, rather than buying and mounting a hanging rack for garden tools, an even simpler no-fuss solution is to simply bang some nails into the wall and hang the tools from them.

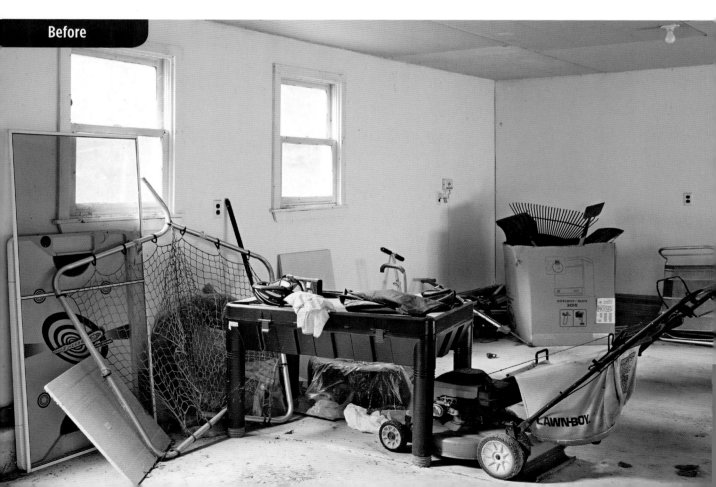

Before

In the After photo below, you can see how we organized the area. We purchased a cheap, easy-to-install wall rack for the long-handled gardening tools. The placement of the gardening tool racks led us to define that back corner as the "gardening/landscape support" area. The lawn mower now has a permanent home on the back wall within this boundary. The new shelf in this same back corner was divided and its various levels were named, devoting two tiers to "gardening/landscape."

Of the remaining three tiers, we dubbed one "auto support" and the last two "beach support." They hold lawn chairs, beach towels, and a radio for the beach. More beach chairs can be hung on the wall just to the left, and Boogie boards are tucked behind the shelves, grouping all beach supplies together.

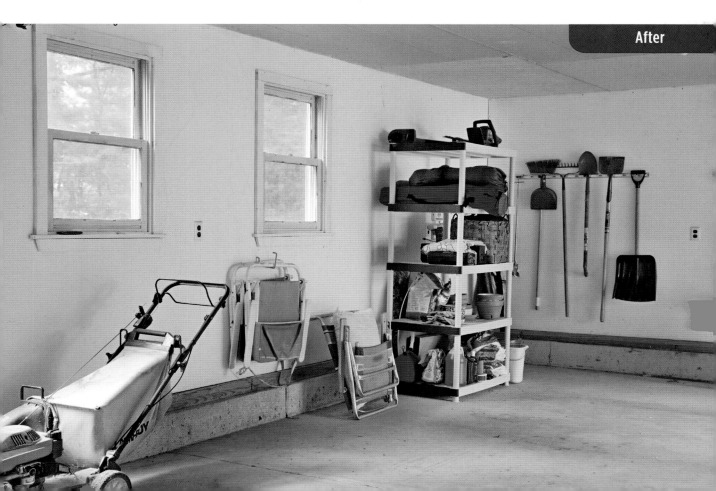

After

The Entry Area to the House

The door from the garage to the house was surrounded by more undefined piles, shown in the Before photo below. Golf clubs on their way to the basement pile up to the right. More lawn equipment, computers that are on their way to donation, and garbage bags that never made it across the garage, litter the floor.

Fast and Furious Tip: Call your town or waste management service if you're looking to replace your garbage can. Often, they provide taller rolling garbage cans free of charge. Use the tallest rolling garbage can your town or service (and your space!) will allow to procure more storage and floor space.

Before

The now-organized entry area to the house, shown in the After photo below, was also renamed. Athletic equipment and lawn care items have been removed, and this space now hosts the "garbage/recycling" area. Large bins capture the recycling, and because the family now has large indoor bins, the chore of taking out recycling has been reduced to dumping the indoor bin over, in one simple motion, once a week on garbage day. Gone are multiple trips with many small inadequate brown paper or plastic bags. A taller garbage can doesn't take up much more footprint than the older one, giving more storage in less space while helping to prevent garbage from overflowing.

The Golf Area

As you can see in the photo to the right, some remaining space along the back wall was given over to golf clubs that were on their way to the basement or that were removed from the basement. Because golf is played outdoors, and golf bags are loaded in the car, efficiency demanded we find a space for the clubs in the garage. Using wall brackets that we purchased, as well as some leftover lumber the family had on hand, we created a "golf" area. The hooks on the bottom of the brackets act as a braces to hold the bags upright. Long nails would have been a no-fuss solution that worked just as well. The top of the braces provides a "golf support" shelf. The bicycle pump migrated up here because the low shelf accommodated its height. Occasionally, boundaries bend a bit to accommodate odd shapes, but because the bikes and the pump are still in the same room and both are easy to access, efficiency hasn't been compromised.

By naming our boundaries and providing adequate containers, this garage went from cluttered mess to a no-fuss efficient space that every family member can use and easily maintain.

We organized one last utility space in this home using our no-fuss method—lots of weeding, creating boundaries, and quick and easy-to-assemble containerization. Let's look at how a simple quick weeding and containerization can make the most of even a small space: the utility closet.

Repurpose What You Have on Hand

We used cannibalized shelves, a leftover garbage can, and some old lumber to organize this garage. By all means, repurpose things you have on hand, but don't be afraid to get rid of those things you don't use or to whittle things down to live within a boundary. One containerization shelf in the basement and half a dozen pieces of lumber are all you need to keep. It is more organized to occasionally reprocure what you might need than to trip over a lot of clutter that you mostly won't need.

A little creativity with some old lumber and some new wall brackets organizes the golf supplies.

5 STEPS

THE UTILITY CLOSET

As you can see in the Before photo below, this family formerly shoved all of their mops and brooms behind a door of the laundry room, which was located right off the kitchen. Because the kitchen had no broom closet (oh dear), drafting a portion of the laundry room for this purpose made sense. But storing the brooms so they lean up against the door means that every time the door is moved, something falls to the floor, tripping anyone who enters. Let's see how our five-step no-fuss method solved this problem and made the space much more efficient and organized.

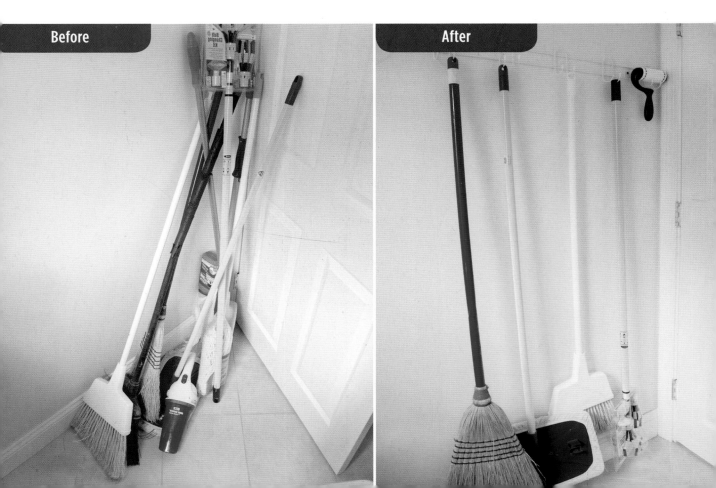

Before

After

STEP ONE

We scheduled a morning for one person to tackle this project. Because the family had researched hanging racks during the recent garage project, we were confident we knew our options. This project was so small that we didn't need to supplement our garbage bags.

STEP TWO

We weeded the brooms and mops down to the old standbys, eliminating the redundancies and novelties. We did keep two brooms—one for indoors and the other for the outside deck.

STEP THREE

The dust buster was removed to its recharging station, near an outlet on an adjacent wall, and the long-handled redundant tools went to the large outdoor trash.

STEP FOUR

We named the wall behind the door "utility tools with handles," creating a boundary that *excluded the floor.*

STEP FIVE

Finally, we purchased a simple rack with hooks that holds the mops and brooms up off the floor. A no-fuss solution of simply banging in some nails to use as hooks was deemed too aesthetically unpleasing in this finished space, but it would have accomplished the same thing while eliminating that extra trip to the hardware store. You can see the results in the After photo to the left.

In all three of the spaces organized in this chapter, getting items up and off the floor and into appropriate shelving or onto the walls moved us toward a more organized space. Our new storage is simple and no-fuss, and because we weeded and sorted possessions first, the need to buy new storage was kept to a minimum. In our next chapter, we'll see how boundaries, appropriate storage, and weeding can transform the living areas of your home just as dramatically.

Fast and Furious Tip: Advertisers will constantly try and convince you that a newer, better broom or mop will save you time and do a better job. Go ahead and try them out if you must, but if you discover that the new broom and mop requires maintenance—accessories, and specialized pieces that add to your burden and budget—then call it a failed experiment and go back to the tried-and-true tools that your grandmother used.

CHAPTER 6

THE LIVING ROOM, FOYER, AND FAMILY ROOM

Before

IF YOUR HOME HAS BOTH a family room and a living room, or just one room in which you entertain and relax as a family, creating boundaries—and living within them—will keep your space free of clutter and available for entertaining and family activities. The home we'll explore in this chapter has both a family room and a formal living room that also serves as the home's foyer. As you can see in the Before photo of the family's living room here, the lack of boundaries for both activities and possessions made the room inefficient to use and maintain.

In this chapter, we'll look at how we can apply our fast and furious, no-fuss five-step method to organizing a living room, a foyer, and a family room. In doing so, we'll look closely at the two steps—failure to weed and name to create boundaries—that most often sabotage these rooms in a home. Let's begin by applying our five steps to the living room.

After

5 STEPS

THE LIVING ROOM

STEP ONE

We scheduled a single six-hour day and two people to organize the living room. We didn't research containerization because my eye was practiced enough to see that this room probably wouldn't need any, but we did check to make sure the family had a sufficient supply of varied plastic bags on hand—white for donations and sturdy large black for garbage.

STEP TWO

As you can see in the Before photo on page 128, most of the items that cluttered this room didn't even officially belong here. Our "other areas" piles included dishes for the kitchen and laundry for the bedrooms. A semi-permanent blue laundry basket of toys (in the right-hand side of the photo) was emptied, and the toys went to the children's rooms. Some books went into a donation bag, and some redundant plants on a windowsill (see Before photo on page 132) were set aside to give away.

STEP THREE

All the "other areas" piles were put away, the donations were taken to the car, and duplicates species and excess plants were placed curbside with a "Free" sign attached to them.

STEP FOUR

We named this room "living room"—*not* snack room, laundry room, playroom, family portrait gallery, children's art gallery, or greenhouse. We determined that a living room was a place for quiet conversation, reading, and adult company. It is the one room in the house whose primary goal is *to look beautiful* and stay that way, always available for entertaining or quite reflections without preparatory fuss. In keeping with the name and boundaries of the room, the shelves and window ledge were given the name "decorative," not storage. Some further weeding was required to stay within this aesthetic boundary.

Allowing children to store their toys in every room of the house turns any home into a cluttered and chaotic space that sabotages *everyone's* comfort.

STEP FIVE

With weeding and boundaries, no containers were necessary in this room. However, often living room clutter can be eliminated through the addition of a single finished bookcase to hold decorative items, photos, and books.

The Results and Our No-Fuss Solutions

Naming the space to create boundaries, and *committing* to those boundaries, reclaimed this room by making it efficient to use, as shown in the After photo on page 133. Let's see where efficiency was previously violated and how boundaries got us back on track.

Laundry

Laundry is neither washed in the formal living room, nor are clothes stored there. Bringing the laundry into the living room creates an unnecessary step by adding an *inefficient* side trip. It also eliminates much of the motivation for family members to put away their clean laundry. If each family member's laundry had been sorted on the bed in their respective bedrooms, then folded laundry would by necessity be put away before bedtime.

FIVE TIPS FOR FAMILY PHOTOS

1. Define a "family photo gallery" space in your home—the wall of the stairwell, the upstairs hallway, or a decorative shelf in the living room, and confine *all* family photos within that boundary.

2. Avoid having many small frames, which creates clutter. Fewer large frames honor the aesthetics of your home *and* the subject of the photo.

3. Use matching frames to keep photo groupings looking cohesive and uncluttered.

4. Whenever possible, choose to display photos on a wall, not a surface. Photos on a flat surface make it inefficient to dust and can add to the feel of clutter.

5. Avoid large frames with a pre-cut matte for many photos. Finding photos that are the right size and orientation and that look good together is a tedious project you don't need.

Toys

Families with young children often work to make their home "child friendly" without considering that what they may truly wish to do is make the home "family friendly." In this room, removing the children's toys and art from the adult entertainment area, and prohibiting them from snacking here, is the fast and furious method to an easy-to-clean, efficient-to-maintain, restful retreat for *everyone*.

Shelves: Books, Photos, and Decorative Objects

As you can see in the Before photo to the left, books, photos, and decorative objects overwhelmed the available shelving, creating a hard-to-maintain space. And books and cabinetry couldn't be accessed without first moving more framed pictures aside. Furthermore, many of the photos couldn't even be seen because other photos were obscuring them. The entire purpose of the decorative shelving—to look attractive—was sabotaged by *too many* attractive items. To reclaim a calming aesthetic, we needed to ruthlessly limit decorative objects—no matter how beautiful—in number, color, and scale.

As shown in the After photo to the right, our no-fuss solution was to give each shelf its own individual boundary—bookshelf, picture shelf, decorative object shelf. Of course, an interior decorator would mingle the items on the shelves, but this family, like so many others, couldn't call on the specialized skills of an interior decorator. And they had firsthand evidence that attempting to intermingle on their own resulted in a cluttered mess.

Before

The boundary of the family photo gallery was reduced to two shelves of favorite pictures that were large enough to match the scale of the shelf, and of a size and design that coordinated well with each other and the back of the shelf. All the small framed and loose pictures were removed.

As you can see in the After pictures of the living room below and on page 129, the room has been transformed into a peaceful, easy-to-maintain, family-friendly space. This room is now available for entertaining, perusing the Sunday paper, reading a special book to one of the children, and as a spot for the family to gather when they just want to enjoy each other's company. Notice that to achieve our goals, *no money was spent on new storage or furnishings*. Everything was accomplished fast and furiously with weeding and boundaries.

> **Fast and Furious Tip:** Limit the number of framed photos on surfaces and the number of plants on the floor. This will cut down on your dusting and ease your vacuuming chores, leaving your home cleaner, more beautiful, and easier to maintain.

After

5 STEPS

THE FOYER

The Before photo shown below reveals that this living room is also the main entry to the home, so the one function we could not weed out is that of foyer. Let's see how we used our five steps to organize this small entryway so that it functions efficiently for the family, yet doesn't overwhelm the rest of the room.

Before

STEP ONE

Because everyone uses this space, we scheduled three hours for two adults, with the children chipping in to help weed for the first hour. We also did some brainstorming and preliminary Internet research on shoe racks.

STEP TWO

Without an entry closet (the door in the picture leads to another room) the available storage consisted of twelve hooks and a newel post. Consequently, everyone in the family, even the youngest child, was asked to weed the bags down to one backpack, schoolbag, or beach bag per child, one purse for mom, and one laptop case for dad. Coats, hats, and mittens were weeded down to a single hat and two pairs of mittens/gloves per family member, and coats were pared to three per person.

STEP THREE

Excess shoes and bags were removed to their owners' bedrooms. Excess outerwear in good condition was donated.

After

STEP FOUR

We expanded the boundary of the foyer to officially include the newel post and a white chest on the opposite side of the door. Videos were removed from the chest (efficiency dictates that we place them near the TV) so that it could be co-opted as storage for puffy winter coats. In this space we used "grandmother's method" to store accessories—mittens went into coat pockets, and winter hats and scarves down the sleeve of the owner's coat—a solution that is eminently practical. Drafting the newel post was an ugly but sensible storage solution. As long as we define the boundary as one item (one bag), when company comes, it is easy enough to transfer that item to a hook.

STEP FIVE

We bought and assembled a shoe rack to increase storage using vertical space. Everyone was assigned one tier and would be responsible for keeping their downstairs shoe inventory to a number that fit on that tier, with space left over for the shoes of one guest. For Mom and Dad, that means two pairs each; the kids can fit three pairs each, with taller boots and galoshes on top.

A shoe rack provides a visual boundary for how many shoes each family member is allowed to keep by the door.

The Results and Our No-Fuss Solutions

Notice in our After photo shown to the left, that by grouping Mom and Dad's longer coats over the shoe rack, and keeping the shorter items on the other wall, we have uncovered the lower bank of hooks. Giving the children easy access to these hooks is crucial in this small space.

As for maintenance, when company comes, the item from the newel post can be easily cleared to double up on the wall hooks, shoes that have been kicked off and left on the floor can be quickly plopped on the shelf, and the lid of the chest dropped down to the closed positions, all in under ten seconds. And although open hooks will never be as attractive—especially in a formal space—as closed closet doors, they do provide a no-fuss storage system that your child will always find easier to use than a hanger.

FIVE TIPS FOR ORGANIZING YOUR COAT CLOSET

1. Weed to three. Almost anyone can get by, no matter the climate, with three coats—a puffy winter ski–style coat, a trench coat for rainy days and formal occasions, and a spring/fall windproof jacket.

2. Avoid the seasonal switch. Outerwear of all seasons should be kept to a number that will fit comfortably in your coat closet, eliminating forever the inefficient and time-consuming "seasonal switch."

3. Get rid of all those multiple scarves and hat/mitten sets you received as gifts. When items need replacing, you can reacquire in the latest fashions and colors.

4. If you have room, buy a slew of inexpensive, neutral color, matching, one-size-fits-all, non-hand-specific gloves for cold (not snowy) days that can be worn by *all* the children. When every glove is the same size, fits both hands, can be worn by anyone, and matches every other, the orphan mitten hunt is forever eliminated.

5. Place shoebox-style bins on a coat closet shelf, one per family member, to define the boundary of hat/mitten/scarf inventory.

THE FAMILY ROOM

Many modern homes boast a living room, a family room, and a playroom—three rooms in which to recreate, entertain, and relax. One would think that this would be more than enough space to pursue family activities without creating clutter. Yet again and again, I walk into homes that are stuffed to the rafters with excess clutter, in which every activity and variety of inventory bleeds into every space, and in which every family member is unhappy and frustrated with the state of the home. Whether your home has all three of the aforementioned rooms, or only one room to serve all of the above functions, violating boundaries will result in an inefficient, chaotic space.

In our spotlight home, there was no playroom. The family room must host a select number of toys while the bulk of the toys will remain in the children's bedrooms. It is then critical to organize this family room in such a way that the end of the day "toy pick-up" is a no-fuss, fast and furious activity that allows every family member to enjoy the space.

In the Before photo shown to the left, you can see what happens if a room serves too many functions supported by too much stuff. The room has become so cluttered that some Christmas decorations were "missed" in the after-Christmas cleanup and are still malingering in the space. Office items and paperwork, and some children's crafts, litter the coffee table. An outsize supply of firewood and fireplace accoutrements take up a large footprint. A second coffee table, shoved up against the wall, appears to be a catchall for pictures, books, magazines, and general chaos.

Before

In another Before view, shown in the photo on the following page, we see that although the toys have been "containerized" in bins, the system is inefficient in myriad ways. The bins themselves wastefully take up floor space footprint without providing height for vertical storage. The depth of the bins encourage mess making because they force the children to throw things "overboard" as they look for the desired toy at the bottom. Toys with many parts become impossible to use as it is too problematic to find all of their parts in the jumble of several bins.

Fast and Furious Tip: If you can dedicate one room of your house as the playroom, then that is where all the toys belong, with the exception of a handful of very special (expensive, delicate, or not required to share) toys for the bedrooms. If you cannot dedicate a room as a playroom and the family room must host toys, then we reverse the distribution and the bulk of the toys belong in the bedroom while a handful of the *most often played with* toys can stay in the family room.

5 STEPS

THE FAMILY ROOM

Let's see how we used our fast and furious five-step approach to turn this family room into a functional, efficient, and organized space.

STEP ONE

We scheduled an eight-hour day for the family to come together and address this room. A small amount of Internet research gave us pricing on shelves and bins.

Before

STEP TWO

Each child was told to weed their toys for the broken, unwanted, unusable-due-to-missing parts, redundant, and developmentally obsolete. (For more information on how to help your children weed their toys, see pages 150–151.)

Decorative objects were weeded to a number that would look attractive on the mantel, and magazines were weeded to a number that would fit in one magazine rack. Firewood was weeded to the amount that would fit in the fireplace. All of the DVDs and videos were moved from elsewhere in the home and gathered together with other media under the TV, and then they were weeded down to a single media: DVDs. Videos were tagged for donation.

Fast and Furious Tip: Avoid massive unwieldy collections of Barbie dolls, Matchbox cars, action figures, or stuffed animals. After all, children only have two hands. And when friends visit, learning to share the limited supply of dolls, or draft a stuffed animal into the game, improves creativity *and* social skills.

After

The large pink floor pillow was eliminated from the floor in front of the TV. Although the children did lounge there, it was a space hog, gobbling up all available floor space in the "play area" and unnecessarily duplicating the function of the couch.

STEP THREE

Donations were removed to the car. The paperwork was removed to the office to abide within its own efficient boundaries. Excess children's toys were removed to their bedrooms. Christmas items were stowed.

STEP FOUR

Following the dictates of how the space has been traditionally used, activity boundaries were named. A playroom area was defined on the left side of the room. The right side of the room was defined as a TV viewing and conversation area.

To organize the children's possessions within the new boundary, each child was given a set amount of floor space for storing their toys. After naming these boundaries, it was obvious that despite weeding, more and better storage was needed for the youngest child's toys and for the DVDs.

STEP FIVE

Two inexpensive, prefabricated, easy-to-assemble shelves containerize the toys and DVDs, respectively, and required less than an hour to throw together. Some bins and open front baskets on the shelves helped to further organize the toys.

Fast and Furious Tip: If you only *occasionally* light a fire, buy a single bunch of firewood and store it within the fireplace. Replenish only as needed at your local grocers.

The Results and Our No-Fuss Solutions

In the After photos on pages 139 and 141, you can see the results of our labors. Notice that the extra coffee table is gone. The orange chair has been removed from the children's play area where it didn't belong, and it has been repositioned across from the sofa to help create a conversational area. A floor lamp was added behind the chair, and a magazine rack was placed on the floor to the side so that the chair can also serve as a reading area. The number of magazines now has a boundary in the volume that can fit within the magazine rack. By standing the magazines (rather than piling them) and always placing the newest to the front, when the rack fills, the homeowner can grab a handful from the back and discard them.

Each adult kept a couple of favorite DVDs, but the idea of owning a "collection" was rejected. Only the children, who will watch the same movies multiple times, kept a comprehensive library of DVDs, although even these were weeded down to a number that fit in the storage tower.

SIX TIPS FOR ORGANIZING MOVIES AND MUSIC

1. Don't reinvent the wheel. A simple bookcase makes CDs and DVDs easy to remove and easy to restore. (That's why video stores use them.)

2. Reject categories of "jazz" or "action movie." A roughly alphabetical system is a simple no-fuss solution that allows everyone to easily and independently locate and file their choice.

3. Eliminate dated media systems. If you have DVDs, the VHS tapes should go. If you can order movies through your cable server, DVDs should go.

4. Eliminate duplications. If you've copied your CD onto a computer, back it up and donate the original.

5. Remember that you are not the video store. Use a lending library or rental system for DVDs, and let the retailers manage the headache of their storage and organization.

6. Keep in mind "time" clutter. Although downloading music eliminates CD clutter, there is still a price to be paid in "time" clutter.

A shelf organizes toys in this family room.

In the After photo on page 141, you can see that we placed the remote controls in a basket under the TV. Typically, the basket will rest on the end table next to the couch, but a space is reserved for them under the TV on those rare occasions when company is coming.

The oldest child has used all of her floor space boundary for one large toy (the electronic guitar and drum set) that hooks up to the TV. The youngest child required a shelf for her collection of toys. If you look closely at the shelf, shown in the photo to the left, you can see some simple, no-fuss organizing solutions that even a three-year-old can maintain. Open-front baskets make it easy to see every piece of a toy collection without dumping and make it even easier to put a toy away in the correct container with one single motion. Large toys can just be "plopped" on the shelf.

We have also placed a small footstool near the bookshelf. Although it is invisible in this photo, its placement allows the three-year-old the independence to easily grab and put away her toys. Within a couple of years, the stool will be unnecessary.

The top of the bookshelf has been given over to family games. The three year old can't reach these shelves, even with her stool, and "games" fits within the boundary of our name, "toy shelf."

How Many Toys Is Enough?

While we were doing the photo shoot for this room, one of the publishing staff—herself the mother of a young child living in a small space—queried if these were really enough toys (and yes, she had already seen the child's bedroom, where the bulk of her toys were stored). I asked her to think back on her own childhood. A generation ago, there were no playrooms or family rooms. A basement rec room consisted of a bar and a pool table for adults. Our toys were confined to our bedrooms and consisted of a few shelves or a single toy box. Yet, as the tail end of the baby boomer generation, we were the most materialistically rich generation of children to ever hit the planet, and collectively remember our childhoods with a rosy nostalgic glow that has dominated every public medium. So I ask you, as I asked her, is this child, who owns more than an entire schoolroom of children a generation ago, *really* suffering a cruel deprivation of toys? Does the current generation benefit by having so many toys? Can there be too much of a good thing?

Transforming this family room from a chaotic mess to an attractive, easy-to-maintain and functional space required more than just neatly arranging everything on a bookshelf. If we had merely picked everything up, or added more storage, the room would have returned to its former chaos within a week or two. The family had to commit to a *lifestyle* change. They have less stuff, but it's easier to maintain. They are no longer hijacked by clutter, and, most importantly, their lives are now centered on family activities rather than possessions. It could be that this kind of transformation is worth the sacrifice of some broken, obsolete, or redundant toys.

Fast and Furious Tip: For safety's sake, bolt tall shelves to the wall, especially in a home with young children.

SIX TIPS FOR AN ORGANIZED FAMILY ROOM

Even people without children can find the family room a difficult space to organize. I find some of the same challenges in many of these homes, so here are a few tips to follow:

1. Place low-backed swivel chairs between the couch and television so that they can do double duty for television viewing and conversation.

2. Use end tables, sofa tables (behind the couch), and coffee tables so that the occupant of every seat has a place—other than the floor—to set down his or her drink.

3. Place an end table with a drawer near the seating area. The drawer can be used as a "home" for the remote controls.

4. Place a large basket behind the couch to catch throw blankets.

5. Place adequate shelving near the television to store DVDs and electronic equipment.

6. Place the television over or next to the fireplace (even if the hearth isn't a working fireplace) so that seating can be arranged around a single focal point.

CHAPTER 7

THE CHILDREN'S BEDROOM AND CLOSET

Before

After

SOME TIME AGO, I had a client who professed to love her daughter too much to throw out any of her toys, schoolwork, or art. This eight-year-old hadn't invited a friend to play at her home for over a year because both mother and daughter were too ashamed of the clutter. As parents, we must do that which is in our child's best interest. Just as we don't let them play in traffic, we shouldn't retain toddler toys until they reach college age. Unfortunately, time and again, I see children's bedrooms that are cluttered by an overabundance of toys or a storage system that is inefficient and difficult for a child to maintain.

In the Before photo shown here, you can see an example of a typical three-year-old's bedroom. In this chapter, we'll see how we used our no-fuss, fast and furious five-step method to organize both this child's bedroom and closet.

> **Fast and Furious Tip:** In a young child's room, put decorative items up high where they can be admired but not touched.

THREE TIPS FOR FAST AND FURIOUS CHILDREN'S BEDROOM CLEANUP

1. Place an open laundry basket–style hamper in your child's bedroom to allow him or her to toss in dirty clothes in one simple motion.

2. Add a wastebasket. I have yet to see a child trot down the hall to dispose of a used facial tissue in the bathroom waste can.

3. Limit the blankets to a puffy comforter. Even young children can make the bed if the job consists of nothing more than pulling up a puffy comforter to hide an imperfectly straightened sheet.

THE CHILDREN'S BEDROOM

STEP ONE

Given that this is the bedroom of a very young girl, we scheduled a day when the child would be away from home. Even if parents are on board, very young children may find it difficult to let go of any toys—even those they have clearly outgrown. So Step One, when applied to the reorganization of a very young child's room, does not necessarily require that the child be present. However, this child's parents did prepare her for the change by telling her that she was going to get some new furniture and have a pretty new "big girl" room. As usual, before the scheduled day, we double-checked our plastic bag inventory and familiarized ourselves with the container options.

STEP TWO

In a home with a separate playroom, Mom and Dad's life will be forever easier if we limit the number of toys that are kept in the bedroom. One or two special or expensive toys that your child is reluctant to share, a bookcase for nighttime reading, and a couple of stuffed animals (no more than three!) for the bed will make cleaning your child's room a breeze for either parent or child. In this child's home, however, there was no playroom, so the bulk of the child's toys have to be stored in her bedroom.

We pawed through a series of bins on the floor at the foot of the bed to see what could go. Out went all the large baby toys that were no longer developmentally appropriate. The broken, obsolete, and "pieces missing" toys were also removed. Some redundancies were eliminated. A large collection of baby books—some of them going back to Mom's childhood—that were inaccessibly crammed into a low shelf were reduced because the local library is within walking distance. Along with the books, baby clothes were placed in donation bags.

The oversized "space hog" toys—a shopping cart, a pink car riding toy, a play kitchen, a baby stroller, and a rocking horse—were examined with a particularly critical eye. Only the most beloved would make the cut. The shopping cart, which was being used as a storage container for an overwhelmingly large collection of play food, was eliminated. The toy food collection was then reduced to a size that fit within the cabinetry of the play kitchen.

STEP THREE

The pink car was removed to the garage, where someday soon it will be replaced by a tricycle. Donation and garbage bags were removed to the car and the trash bins.

STEP FOUR

We named each space and returned this little girl's possessions to her room within boundaries. We named the closet as "little girl's wardrobe," so Mom's overflow, out-of-season clothing, and extra linens were banished. The child's clothes went into the bureau or were hung in the now roomy closet. Her shoes and slippers were lined up on the closet floor, and her winter blanket was placed on the closet shelf above her clothes. However, the toys still littered the bedroom floor as a low decorative shelving unit patently did not provide enough storage.

STEP FIVE

To get the toys up and off the floor, we needed to invest in better containerization. We procured a *tall*, white, easy-to-assemble prefabricated bookshelf as well as some open-front baskets and clear bins. We were also able to draft some baskets and containers—a yellow plastic basket and a rattan basket—that were already in the home to further containerize toys on the shelf.

Fast and Furious Tip: If you have small children, consider placing their books *upright* (not stacked) in a small bin. This clever trick is from Kathy Waddill, author of *The Organizing Sourcebook*. Children can't read titles on the spine, so a presentation that allows them to flip through and see the covers is less frustrating for them. And as children's books come in a variety of unusual shapes, it is easier to drop them in a bin than wrestle them onto a shelf.

The Results and Our No-Fuss Solutions

In the photos shown here, you can see how reducing the toys and improving the storage creates a no-fuss, efficient, easy-to-maintain space. Our little girl's books now fit in two bins—one clear, one rattan—that make them easy to flip through and easy to put away. Various clear and open-front bins corral different toy collections without the extra step of labeling. The bins aren't overcrowded so they never have to be dumped to find a particular piece, and toys can be returned to them in one simple "drop it in" motion.

Rolling toys and the heaviest books are placed on the lowest shelf. A step stool (not pictured) is placed at the foot of the bed to the left of the shelf, so the child can easily access the upper shelves, and Mom can conveniently "toe" the stool under the bed when company is coming. In a matter of a very few years, the step stool will be eliminated altogether. The very top shelf and the top of the bookshelf itself were given the named boundary of "decorative items."

Although this child has fewer toys and clothes than she started with, her room is now a more inviting play space. She needn't wrestle a book from a wobbly, overcrowded, crammed shelf, nor unstack the rocking horse from atop the pink car to use it. Everything is more efficient to use, easier to see, and a breeze to put away. By promoting efficiency over ownership, we have given her a beautiful big-girl room that can host her toys, friends, and imagination.

In Depth: Helping Your Child Weed

How do we cycle toys out of the house while respecting our children's feelings and staying sensitive to their needs? How do we sensitively teach our children to let go of their possessions? How much control should we give them regarding the disposition of their toys?

Obviously, older children and teenagers should have almost complete control over the disposition of their possessions—*so long as they maintain an acceptable level of cleanliness and contain those possessions within their room or other boundary.* (For those who struggle, support may be needed.) By the time children are teens, they should have cleaned and organized enough spaces with you to know that addressing every object with the question "keep or go?" is a part of every cleanup job. You can continue to help them in making good organizational decisions by refusing to allow their possessions to bleed into other areas of the house. If you refuse to store your teenager's tricycle in your garage, allotting him space for only one bike, I guarantee he will choose the five-speed over the trike.

For younger children, who may not yet be developmentally ready for much weeding, keeping the clutter down requires a more sensitive but still committed approach in which we begin by limiting the number of toys that enter the house.

But what to do once the toys are in the house? For one, we can lead by example—the sight of Mom or Dad's possessions, earmarked for donation, sitting in the front seat of the car, and the corresponding trip to the donation drop-box, should be as familiar to your children as a trip to the grocery store. Having set an example, we encourage our children to address their own possessions with the question of "keep or go?" by setting aside an afternoon to "organize the toys" in the weeks leading up to Christmas and birthdays. That way, twice a year, each child will challenge the majority of his or her toys with the question "keep, donate, or toss?"

FIVE TIPS TO CONTROL TOY CLUTTER BEFORE IT BEGINS

1. Talk to Grandma and Grandpa (and other relatives and friends) about their unintentionally harmful habit of always arriving with a gift in hand. Put your foot down and mean it. Encourage activities instead—baking, gardening, and so on.

2. Limit birthday party guests to the child's age plus one. For example, a five-year-old should have only six guests, even if the party venue makes you pay for twelve.

3. Santa might consider leaving a number of toys equal to the child's age. After age twelve, gifts should decrease to less than a handful, although they may be more expensive.

4. Never buy junk at the register. Never impulse-buy toys.

5. Make a pact with your siblings that after each of your children reaches a certain age (such as twelve), aunts and uncles will confine themselves to a monetary gift.

To ease the process, once a child has chosen items for donation, praise him or her for the show of generosity, then put the items immediately into an opaque bag, and at the end of the clean-up, whisk the bag out of their sight. (The lack of a visual reminder spares them the discomfort of forever second guessing their decisions.) Our goal is to instill at a young age the idea that all material goods can be ephemeral. They are appropriate for a time in your life, but you are not bound to them forever. We do this because we recognize that learning to let go is a habit as important to their hygiene, and their future quality of life, as brushing their teeth and clearing their dishes.

> ## Our goal is to turn the act of "letting go" into a sanguine habit for our children rather than a cause for high drama and angst.

In my last book, I further advised parents of young children, when the child isn't present, to make one last sweep through the toys and remove the broken, no longer cherished, and "will never be missed." You are their parent; you know which toys qualify. This one bit of advice stirred some controversy. Critics of this method described feeling violated in their childhood when parents had subjected their possessions to a similar culling. So let me clarify: I do not advocate empowering the insensitive to perform a willy-nilly purging of their child's possessions. What I do recommend is using your knowledge of your child to remove those items that will *never be missed*, or if they are casually noted as missing, won't be seriously lamented. Our goal is to spare the child the tiresome chore of addressing every bibelot and gew-gaw that showed up in a party favor bag, was included in a fast-food meal, or popped out of a vending machine, while passing on to poorer or indigent children those better-quality toys that never grabbed your child's interest and that therefore he or she will never miss.

Fast and Furious Tip: If you have a sensitive child, avoid selling his or her toys in a yard sale or giving them to younger cousins. A no-longer-wanted toy can seem precious in the hands of another child and lead to an uncomfortable bout of "seller's" regret.

THE CHILDREN'S CLOSET

We'll now leave the room of this young child and look instead at the closet of her older sister, shown in the Before photo below. Does the closet shown in the Before photo look efficient to use or easy to maintain? Although we can certainly improve its appearance by folding and sorting the clothing into tall piles, will it stay neat and organized? Or is it likely that the first time our eight-year-old attempts to remove something from the bottom, the piles will list, tip, and begin to devolve back into the large scrum of clothing we see here?

Before

After

Using our fast and furious five-step method, let's tackle this closet and reorganize it for efficiency. Our goal is to install an easy, quick, inexpensive system that will allow this child to access her clothing without contributing to a major mess.

STEP ONE

Because this child was old enough to participate—and indeed we needed her guidance on which clothing still fit her—we set aside a Saturday to organize the closet together. I advised scheduling four hours. A typical child's closet, with the supervision of one parent, should take roughly two hours to weed, with another two to buy and "install" containerization. I also advised the mother to make sure she had an adequate supply of plastic bags on hand for garbage and donations.

STEP TWO

We made the bed to use as a staging area and then proceeded to weed out the old, ill-fitting, knitted-by-Grandma-but-I-don't-like-it-and-won't-wear-it, stained, and too small.

As we dug through the closet, we also found some of Mom's belongings, some toys, and bits of general clutter—old papers, books, and toiletries. We made several "other areas" piles for these items. We also made piles of "keeper" items to be returned to the closet. These included, but were not limited to, piles of t-shirts, long-sleeved shirts, shorts, athletic wear, and linens.

STEP THREE

We removed items to the rooms or spaces in which they belonged. Donations were placed in white plastic bags and were removed to the car. We tossed out the irretrievably frayed or damaged. We then quickly wiped down the shelves and vacuumed the floor.

Fast and Furious Tip: Listen to your children if they say they won't wear something. Then, no matter how expensive, sentimental, or much to *your* taste the item may be, get rid of it.

STEP FOUR

In naming our boundaries, we decided that this closet would be called the "eight-year-old's wardrobe," Notice that we didn't call any space in this closet "toy box," "book shelf," or "the overflow area of mom's things."

In returning the child's clothing to the closet, it quickly became obvious that although her clothing would fit in the closet, it would have to be arranged in tall, unwieldy piles, while her dirty clothes would still float about the floor and become intermingled with her shoes.

STEP FIVE

We agreed that some new forms of containerization would solve our dilemmas, and because we wanted a fast and furious, no-fuss method, we didn't call a custom closet company. Instead we retired to the nearest discount department store where we picked up a series of stacking baskets, an easy-to-assemble shoe shelf, and a laundry basket to be used as a dirty clothes hamper.

Because the contents of the closet had already been weeded and sorted, it took only minutes to rearrange them in the new containers—shoes on the shoe rack, dirty laundry in the hamper, linens (only those that belong on the bed in this room) on the upper shelf, along with a *small* bin with a *very discrete* number of clothes that were too big. Finally, we added stacking baskets to truly transform the closet.

Fast and Furious Tip: By all means keep one or two gift items that your child has yet to grow into, but *do not shop* for next season. Purchase only that which he or she will be able to wear this season. Leave future wardrobe needs for future shopping trips.

The Results and Our No-Fuss Solutions

As you can see in the After photo here, the closet has been transformed into an efficient, organized area. It is now an easy-to-use and no-fuss space to maintain. Stacking baskets provide an easy, inexpensive system for creating multiple small *accessible* piles using vertical space. These baskets are themselves named to create boundaries. (There are separate baskets for t-shirts, long-sleeved shirts, pants, shorts, pajamas, accessories, and ski clothes.) All of the winter and summer wardrobe fits into this one closet so this mother and child will never again have to make the inefficient seasonal switch. Also, by keeping all of the ski clothes—wool socks, long underwear, and polypropylene shirts—together in one bin, we made it easy for this child to prepare for a day of athletics.

Our fast and furious method relies on a "good enough" approach. A series of bins that contain a jumble of t-shirts and only t-shirts, a jumble of pajamas and only pajamas, and a jumble of shorts and only shorts, respectively, is still an organized and efficient space. It may not be as aesthetically appealing as folded piles, but it is organized enough, efficient enough, and maintainable enough to allow this child to access her clothes and put them away in a trice.

Of course, this closet isn't particularly beautiful. It is not made of custom mahogany, and very soon the t-shirts will be a jumble within the t-shirt bin. And although I prefer felt hangers and stacking baskets side by side (not stacked), the confines of the space and our budget compelled us to make some good-enough compromises. The result is a closet that will stay organized enough to function efficiently. Should its owner wish to straighten it up, she will be able to do so in a matter of minutes.

Fast and Furious Tip: For a child's closet, weed out all odd-shaped hangers and rely instead on sturdy, inexpensive white plastic hangers with small hooks. Standardizing hangers is an easy way to greatly improve the aesthetics of a closet and give it the general feeling of an organized space.

CHAPTER 8

THE OFFICE

Before

THE OFFICE, and its ugly spawn, paperwork, is the waterloo of many an otherwise organized homeowner. I caution my clients that organizing paperwork is the most brutal job we will face together. After all, if we were to handle 100 pieces of clothing, we would probably be well on our way to organizing their complete wardrobe. If we handle 100 pieces of paper, we will have addressed less than half an inch of their office!

There are so many ways to inadvertently sabotage the efficiency of an office space. As you can see in the Before photo here, in our spotlight home, a large and comfortable office/guest room has turned into a storehouse for everything from groceries to old paid bills and dated homework.

After

In this chapter, we'll see how a desire to be ultra-organized can lead to organizational Armageddon. We'll do so by looking closely at one family's home office and how our no-fuss five-step method got them back on track. But before we begin, let me caution you that these methods are not the typical advice you'll find in organizing books. These methods are "fast and furious." They will challenge you to be less prepared but more efficient. They will cut down on your paperwork, but occasionally you will have to reacquire information (although less often than when you held on to everything and could find nothing). These methods will rely on resourcefulness. They will promote pragmatism, not perfectionism, reasonable prudence, not paranoia. This is the one area of organizing in which my methods most often completely surprise my clients. But it is also the area in which I most substantially improve their quality of life.

As you read this chapter, you'll notice that in an office, the five no-fuss steps appear more fluid. Although we always weed and sort first, we may start naming categories of paperwork as we go, or we might containerize (file) one category of paper and then go back and weed, name, and containerize another. This is because often the paper project is so big that it naturally breaks down into several smaller organizing projects. Let's get started by looking at how our five-step method turned one office from a cluttered mess into an efficient and welcoming space. We'll first look at the big-picture office space and how it was cleared, and then turn our attention to the paperwork and desktop.

Fast and Furious Tip: Desktops are valuable working real estate. Just as you wouldn't plant zinnias in the vegetable fields that are meant to supply your family with produce, don't litter your desktop with decorative items that impede the flow of paperwork.

5 STEPS

THE BIG-PICTURE OFFICE SPACE

STEP ONE

Two adults and one young teen shared two desks and two computers in this one space, but since most of the clutter belonged to Mom and Dad, we set our calendar around their schedules. It typically takes four to five eight-hour days to weed through the paperwork and reorganize a backlogged home office. Our family scheduled two consecutive weekends and arranged to take off work the Monday of the second weekend, if needed, to complete the job. This may seem like a lot, but given the importance of paying bills and tracking finances, and the resultant stress if these tasks are neglected, isn't a handful of days a bargain price to pay for a well-run home and peace of mind?

Because I have organized so many offices, I also made sure the family had on hand some basic office tools or knew where to quickly procure them. (We'll discuss each object in detail later.)

STEP TWO

On our scheduled day, we began the process of weeding and sorting by tackling the larger items first, proceeding to remove them immediately. It was just more efficient to de-clutter the space and provide some working areas before tackling the paperwork. (We'll discuss how we weeded and sorted the paperwork in just a bit.)

Although limiting the office to paperwork might appear a bit draconian, it provides a family with a restful, efficient environment in which to attend to the high-concentration task of bill paying.

STEP THREE

As noted, we removed all the large items that didn't belong in the office immediately. Bulk shopping purchases (such as the paper towels shown in the Before photo) fell into this easy "remove" category. The family agreed to limit the size of their purchases in the future to a volume that would fit in the room in which the product belonged. An exception was made for crates of water bottles, which were given a shelf in the garage along the path from car to kitchen. At least they no longer make an inefficient side trip to the office. We also removed all of the toys, decorative figurines, novelty gifts, picture frames, and other small bric-a-brac that had worked its way into this space.

STEP FOUR

By now we could see that the next step, "Name to Create Boundaries," was within sight. This room, the office/guest room, would henceforth be used only for paperwork, homework, and, very occasionally, accommodating guests. We allowed for a single exception to these activities: Computer games would continue to be played here, as they require the use of the computer.

STEP FIVE

This room was already well supplied with the larger "containers" (i.e., furniture) that every office needs. All we had to do was clear them of boundary busters and rededicate them to office support. Of course, not every home is so well appointed, but because every modern home *does* need an office space, let's use this section to identify some of the larger items that no efficient home office area can do without.

You will never achieve efficiency if you are working at an antique desk sitting on a hard rickety kitchen chair, nor will your papers every get organized if we don't containerize at least some of them in file drawers. Because efficiency of effort always trumps efficiency of space, if more than two file drawers are needed, I recommend supplementary two-drawer file cabinets rather than tall four-drawer or large lateral file cabinets. The tall units force you to stand up to file a paper, ambushing you into leaving a "to file" pile! The lateral drawers overwhelm with too many visual options, making it harder to find the correct file. A series of two-drawer cabinets will make it easier to create clearer boundaries ("finances" drawer and so on) and provide extended surface area, giving the printer, inbox, and stacking trays convenient and comfortable homes.

The Results and Our No-Fuss Solutions

Before our reorganization, the office shelving and other surfaces didn't support office labors. After we weeded out the jars of coins, bulk shopping, old magazines, empty packaging, and decorative objects, we reclaimed the shelving, desktop, and floor as valuable office support spaces. In the After photo shown on page 159, you see a room that has been transformed in true fast and furious fashion, using mostly the materials at hand. While we've lost a play area and a storage area for bulk shopping, the office has become more efficient because it is now a dedicated space to efficiently and comfortably servicing that most stressful of household tasks—paperwork.

FIVE EASY-TO-ACQUIRE OFFICE FURNISHINGS THAT EVERY HOME NEEDS

1. A desk, with at least one drawer for office supplies and a desktop large enough to hold a computer while leaving room for a writing surface and some desktop tools.

2. One or more two-drawer file cabinets next to the desk to hold paper within and computer peripherals on top.

3. A bookcase or shelving unit next to the desk to hold reference materials, stacking trays, or bins for larger office supplies or computer paraphernalia.

4. Good lighting.

5. A comfortable *rolling* chair.

A FOCUS ON PAPERWORK

Having vanquished the easy stuff, we were now set to look down the belly of the beast—paperwork. Slaying the beast, transforming paper processing into an efficient and fail-proof system, means valuing simplicity over complexity, pragmatism over paranoia, and resourcefulness over preparedness. Ironically, our fast and furious, no-fuss approach has us address the papers in a slap-dash manner to ultimately achieve a more responsible and manageable system.

Weeding and Sorting

We began by weeding and sorting the file drawers. I advise my clients to throw out any obsolete file folders *without looking inside!* It is more efficient to weed an entire file folder in one go than to hunt through its contents of outdated paperwork.

Unfortunately, this perfectionist couple worried that perhaps they had misfiled something important in the wrong folder. Well, maybe they did. But it is also likely that if it was truly important, it had probably already been replaced. Again and again they asked, "But what would it hurt if we just looked through this *one* file?" The answer was, "Looking through one obsolete file doesn't pose a problem. It is the compulsion to look through *every* paper in *every* file that has left you with cartons and piles of unfiled miscellaneous papers all over the desktop and floor, while your file drawers are high-jacked with obsolete papers that require too much effort to throw out." Ironically, it was their very carefulness in processing paper that was causing them to lose track of their current, *most important* paperwork!

Fast and Furious Tip: When weeding files, trust yourself. If the file says "health club information" for a health club you no longer belong to, go ahead and throw the whole file out in one go without rifling through its contents.

Having weeded the existing file folders, we started on the backlog of boxes of papers. "Keeper" papers were sorted into piles like "medical history," "insurance" "vital records" (i.e., birth/death/ marriage certificates) that were either added to existing folders or earmarked as future folders. We kept the latter straight by temporarily labeling the piles with Post-it Notes, keeping the name "fluid" until the sorting process was over. Old bills were tossed, as were old account statements, most of which had never been opened and never would be. The newest statement has the current state of this couple's accounts, and the most current bill states the amount they currently owe. Any desire to go back, correlate, and review is just another example of the perfectionist beast roaring to be fed with more piles of "to do" papers.

We also threw out all redundant copies of papers or hard copies of items on the computer. Maintaining and updating the same information in *two places* is hardly an efficient system.

We continued by weeding out all of the perfectionist penny-pinching paper that was cluttering the office, the house, and my clients' wallets. We weeded out all but two frequent purchaser cards. We threw out the coupon organizer folder along with all of the newspapers that were yet to be looked through for coupons. We also tossed out all the catalogues without looking through them.

Removing the Unwanted

We want to remove things in the quickest way possible, so I advised my clients to get rid of the shredder and just throw out or recycle the bulk of their papers. It is more efficient to drop papers into a recycling basket than to waste time, space, electricity, and fine motor skills carefully feeding things into a shredder. We are a society addicted to our shredders, yet most household documents don't even need to be shredded!

Piles of papers "to be shredded" are just another time-consuming step between clutter and organization.

YOU REALLY DO NOT NEED TO SHRED STUFF

The media has to create content, even on slow news days, and horror stories on identity theft are one of their favorite fillers. Many people are so fearful that they shred anything with their address on it (something many of us publish in the phone book), any bills telling how much they owe (why is it a state secret that you owe fifty bucks to the water company?), anything that has a series of x's followed by the last four digits of account numbers (the first numbers are x'ed out to protect your info, shredding is redundant), anything with a bank account number on it (it's on the bottom of your check every time you hand it to the felon who's behind the cash register at the store), and anything with a credit card number (which can be copied by the server when you hand it over at a restaurant).

We all regularly supply this information to strangers, but then go on to laboriously shred this same information out of fear that the garbage man gives a hoot about our spending habits. As for theft, there is only a miniscule chance that an identity thief is a stranger rifling through your garbage. Truly sophisticated crooks are cyber thieves, and according to a report by the Identity Theft Resource Center, almost 50 percent of identity thefts are committed by someone who the victim knows.

This doesn't mean that you shouldn't be prudent, just that you probably don't need a shredder. If it bothers you to think of your credit card bills and bank statements in the garbage or recycling bin, tear the document in half through the account number, throwing half in the garbage and the other half in the recycling bin. In this way, caution is married to the smallest investment of time and effort.

The one number for which you *should* demonstrate extra care is your social security number. It is printed on about ten papers a year, all of them tax documents, and it can be protected simply and quickly by using a marker (so much more space saving than a shredder!) to cross out the number, followed by tearing the paper in half—through the number—and throwing half in the garbage and the other half in the recycling bin.

Losing the paranoia along with the shredder frees up floor space, and, more importantly, the time and effort it takes to dispose of your papers and maintain the shredder.

Many readers will be concerned about this advice. But if your home contains piles of "to be shredded" paperwork, along with boxes of papers, if you're behind on bills, and your current paperwork is misplaced, then you're probably being *too careful*, with your information, and you are in danger of losing those documents that *are* important among the piles of papers that are obsolete but that you are still micromanaging. For you, the inefficiency inherent in using a shredder is part of the problem, not the solution.

However, if your paperwork is organized and each day's worth of shredding is done by the end of that day, and you're not too far behind on housework and other projects, then you're managing well despite the inefficiency of the shredder, and there really is no need to change your inefficient system.

Handling Files

Having weeded and removed the excess paperwork in the office, we turned our attention to managing the paperwork that remained. As you can see in the Before photo below, the old file drawers were overstuffed, many containing over thirty identical file folders, making the drawers stressful to view and access.

Fast and Furious Tip: Replace old folders with a variety of colorful file folders—but don't color-code. *Randomly* using a variety of colors requires no extra work and provides a small mnemonic aid. Eventually, your eye will go directly to the "insurance" file because you will remember it is the yellow one toward the back of the drawer.

Before

Our new file drawer, shown in the After photo here, is *much easier to use*. By returning only twelve to fifteen files per drawer, we have given the eye half the work of reading to find the correct file folder. By reducing the volume of papers in the drawer, we have made it easier for the hand to slip a paper in a folder with one simple motion. By using a variety of colors, we have given the brain an efficient mnemonic aid for those most frequently used folders.

As we moved on to permanently naming our files, our perfectionist homeowner brought out his newly purchased label maker. We decided to see who could make labels for the folders the fastest. His wife called out "ready, set, go," and both of us raced to make a readable label. My bold capital letters written directly onto the file folder tab with a black felt-tip pen were long since drying while he was still waiting for his label to print. Label makers may produce beautiful labels, but they require batteries, refill tape, printing, cutting down to size, peeling, and centering. Capital letters written with a felt-tipped pen directly on a file folder provide a no-fuss method for labeling files with efficiency.

After

Notice that in doing so we didn't use plastic tabs on hanging folders. These hard to use, time-consuming tabs give no advantage over the handwritten tabs on the file folders themselves. Making a label marked "insurance" and placing it on a hanging folder, followed by five or six files labeled "renters insurance," "car insurance," "health insurance," "dental insurance," etc. forces us, every time we open a file drawer, to read a novel when a poem would suffice. A single file folder marked "insurance policies" can easily hold the four or five policies you have. Once a year, when the new policy arrives, it's a relatively simple matter to pull out the old and replace it with the new.

> Our goal is to make *staying* organized easy. *Filing* papers should require the least amount of effort, *even if* that adds an extra couple of seconds when it comes time to retrieve papers.

Remember that we are striving for efficiency. Fewer files make it easier to file. If we put up a series of perfectionist roadblocks to filing a paper (finding the label maker, threading a plastic tab into the hanging folder, creating a separate file for every paper that needs to be filed, indexing our files), papers will eddy out in "to be filed" piles, where they *will* get lost. As always, ease of putting something away takes preference over ease of retrieval. Still, it is neither stressful nor unduly time consuming to rifle through a file folder if you're confident that the paper you seek is in there. In files that grow too thick, you can weed the next time you rifle, tossing obsolete paperwork efficiently as you go.

Fast and Furious Tip: In naming files, *never* use generalities like "important," "urgent," or "current." Be specific: "divorce" *not* "legal documents"; "vital records" (birth/death/marriage certificates) *not* "important papers"; "taxes" and the *specific* year *not* "current taxes." A "current taxes" file has to be regularly weeded or its contents transferred and re-named, but a "taxes 2010" folder is correctly labeled from its creation until the moment the entire folder and contents can be thrown away.

For our homeowners, we found several ways to consolidate files. Instead of three files for the title of each of their *three* cars, and another three folders for the repairs bills on each car, and another three folders for the insurance policies of said cars, we placed their insurance policies together into an "insurance policy" folder with other policies, recycled their repair bills, and placed all of the titles in a folder marked "deeds and titles" that also holds the title to the house. We took *more than nine folders* and turned them into two.

> **Fast and Furious Tip:** Most file drawers can be arranged alphabetically, a system that makes filing simple and efficient.

FIVE FILES YOU CAN ELIMINATE

1. Health History: Unless you are in the middle of a complicated multi-doctor crisis, rely on your doctor's medical records to keep track of your history. You need only retain a copy of your child's last physical for sports teams and camps.

2. Car maintenance: the next owner only cares about the blue book value, not the repair history, which your mechanic has in his computer in any case.

3. Fitness: The paper outlining your yoga exercises should be posted on the wall near your yoga mat until the movements are memorized. Any other information can be found on the Web when you need it.

4. Craft/hobby/decorating/renovating ideas: You are not a reference library, but you are resourceful enough to find ideas at the library or on the internet when you imminently need them.

5. Recipes/possible travel destinations/local services: Likewise, use the library or the internet when your need is imminent.

Containerizing Paperwork

Let's look in depth at some of the decisions we made to containerize the office paperwork. As you'll see, this family found a compromise in their office that allowed them to be efficient while retaining some aesthetic standards. They did a fast and furious reorganization, using the materials at hand, while rejecting an "even better" perfectionism of preparedness.

Corralling photos in one place will keep them safe and prevent them from contributing to the clutter.

The Bookshelf

As you can see in the Before photo shown below, the office bookshelf used to be a cluttered mess. By making the following few small changes, we turned it into the clean and orderly space shown in the After photo:

- We placed a large brown basket for recycling papers to the left of the middle shelf in the After photo.

- Also on this shelf, we placed a floral box in which the family can save one or two pieces a year of the younger child's artwork and any autobiographical homework.

- We drafted two matching striped cloth-covered boxes that the homeowners already owned, to hold investment reports from two different firms, and then placed them on the lower shelf. The homeowners can throw out the bottom layers of statements without looking as the box fills up.

- Because the boxes match, we did a quick labeling (unlike the floral art box, which is distinctive enough to stand out on its own). Instead of using confusing general euphemisms such as "financial statements," we labeled each box with the name of the investment firm.

- We placed a smaller box labeled "Photos 2011–" on the bottom shelf as well. When the box fills, it will be given an end date and a new box can be started.

- We set a box labeled "printer paper" beneath the printer in the remaining box on the lowest shelf. In a bid for efficiency over beauty, I suggested that (a) the printer paper sit on the shelf next to the printer—you can see a stack I placed there to the left—and that (b) all of the boxes in the shelving unit be left open with their lids underneath, making it easier to "wing" things into them. The lids could be easily plopped back on top when guests arrive. I further suggested that (c) both investment reports go into one box. So long as the newest report is on the top, the reports would still be filed chronologically. On the first two suggestions, I was overruled on the basis of aesthetics, for the third suggestion, I was overruled on the basis of perfectionism.

Bill Paying Containers

In a former age, everyone kept their old paid bills because it was the only record of how much they had been charged. Today, if we want to know how much we paid for water last year, we can find out with one quick call or login to the water company. We don't need to keep our paid bill paperwork.

> The most efficient system for paying bills is a paperless one that relies on the computer.

WHY YOU NEED BOTH A GARBAGE CAN AND A PAPER-RECYCLING BIN

Every office needs a garbage can separate from the paper-recycling bin. If your town doesn't recycle paper, then think of these as a trash can for plastic packaging, facial tissues, etc. and a waste paper bin. A large recycling bin, conveniently located next to the desk, allows everyone to throw out paperwork *that they probably won't need* with a feeling of confidence. This is how we fight the perfectionist beast that is always worried about "needing it again some day." A deep bin takes six months or so to fill (because it stores papers flat). Consequently, people who are reluctant to let go of papers can do so with confidence knowing that, if a paper needs to be retrieved, there is a six-month grace period during which it is still in the house, "filed" chronologically, in the recycling bin.

However, my clients were reluctant to throw out the paid bill paperwork, so instead we created a fast and efficient container system. We set aside one drawer, named "household accounts." We then labeled twelve folders by month. Any bill that was paid in January, no matter when it arrived, went into the "January" folder. February bills went into the "February" folder, and so on. In this way, at the end of each twice-monthly bill paying chore, instead of laboriously filing each bill separately (phone bill to phone bill file, water bill to water bill file—sheesh!), the entire pile of paid bill paperwork was all just dumped together willy-nilly, in one simple motion, into the file folder of that month. In homes that wish to retain financial statements and bank statements (not necessary), but are willing to forego the "perfectionist" system of separate boxes used by this family, the monthly files can also hold that month's bank or financial statement. That way, at bill paying time, the filing chore will consist of filing almost all of the paperwork (with the occasional exception of tax documents) easily, efficiently, and quickly, in one simple motion in just one single file!

In a year my clients will dump the dated January bills (in your home this might include the statements as well) without review, into the garbage, so that the folder becomes available for the current January paid bills paperwork. At the front of the drawer, we put a current tax folder *marked with the year.* Any cancelled checks to charities, acknowledgements from charities of donations, or credit card bills that showed charitable contributions, along with all other tax documents, will get dropped directly into this folder so that it is all assembled when it is time to work on taxes.

Fast and Furious Tip: Place a paper recycling bin, one per child, beneath the desks of your older students. The bin starts empty in September, then all year long, completed homework is dumped within. The bin itself isn't dumped out until June. This system gives students a comfort level that encourages them to clean their binders, tossing old paperwork because they are protected on the off chance that they will unexpectedly discover a need to look back at an old unit.

Mail Sorting Containers

Using stacking trays as our containers, we also set up a mail sorting system like the one shown in the photo below. Upon arrival, all mail is sorted, *unopened*, into stacking trays. Colored file folders named with a felt-tip pen—"bills to be paid," "statements," and, if necessary, "charity,"—can be placed in the stacking trays as labels. These labels are "upside down" as the file folder has a different orientation to the reader than a file in a drawer. Notice that the bills and statements are unopened and are placed *on top* of the folders (not within them). The folders are merely being used as a convenient labeling device that allows the homeowners to vertically stack and organize their unopened mail in one simple motion.

On bill paying day, the homeowners take their two to three stacks. They pay their bills, and when they are done, they dump the one pile of "paid bill" paperwork into one single folder—the one with the current month.

Stacking trays allow you to sort mail unopened into organized vertical piles.

Bank Statement Containers

When going through bank statements, all you really need to do is open them up and run a quick eyeball over them. If everything looks about right, *they can be thrown out*. After all, they are just a snapshot to keep you updated, and all of this information is online.

However, my client was a "what if" worrier, so we found a way to containerize his bank statements simply and quickly in a mesh basket on a shelf next to the computer area, as shown in the photo below. We also set up containers for the large financial statements that come from investment firms and brokerage houses. These containers took the form of two decorative boxes on the bottom shelf of the white bookcase, also shown in the photo below. When the boxes grow full, the homeowners can empty out the bottom half in one quick dump and still retain a year's worth of records. The tax documents that come from these same firms at the end of the year—and which are clearly marked as "tax information" on the envelope—go directly into the current (marked with the year) tax folder.

Charity and Tax Containers

My clients only receive a few charitable solicitations by mail each month, so instead of using a separate tray, they throw these in with "bills to be paid." If there is enough money left over at the end of bill paying, my clients may choose to give money to a charity. If not, they throw out the charity requests without looking at them. They may also discover that some of the charity mail is an acknowledgement of a donation. These they drop into the current (marked with the year) tax file.

Toward the end of the year, the homeowners will start to receive tax documents in the mail from the government, investment firms, and employers. This mail is sorted unopened into the "statements" shelf of the mail sorting center. At bill-paying time, they are dumped unopened into the tax file, organized with their other tax information awaiting the one afternoon a year when they put together their taxes.

FIVE TIPS FOR CUTTING BACK ON MAIL-GENERATED PAPERWORK

1. Do own two credit cards, but only use one so you reduce the number of bills you have to pay.

2. Don't open accounts at department stores to get the discount (another bill to pay! more junk mail! more coupons to track!).

3. Cancel department store accounts and ask them to take you off their mailing lists.

4. Limit magazine subscriptions to one weekly and one monthly. When the magazine rack fills up, throw out everything but the two most recent.

5. Consider reducing your investments to one firm, especially if you never open statements. Investment firms are notorious for generating paperwork. If you are not tracking them carefully in any case, simplifying to a single firm might encourage you to stay on top of your finances.

A FOCUS ON THE DESK AREA

Let's closely examine some of the areas in this office to see how we containerized our paper processing systems in the physical space. We started by clearing the cluttered desktop shown in the Before photo below of decorative items and replaced them with useful office tools.

Ongoing Projects Stacking Trays

In our After picture, shown on the next page, the decorative items are gone, the desktop is more useful, and because it is uncluttered, it is *more* attractive. We've added a set of stacking trays to the right that corral various projects. For instance, our homeowners like to hold off on paying their medical bills because the full charge is usually sent to their home before their insurance company gets around to reimbursing the doctor. So one of the stacking trays corrals the unpaid medical bills and holds them until they can be reconciled with the deleterious insurance statements. Another tray holds all of the paperwork for a volunteer project that will last throughout the school year. In your home, the use of these stacking trays will be specific to your life and interests.

Before

Stacking trays allow you to pile frequently referred to papers on your desk, vertically, organized, and distinct from other papers. When a project comes to an end, the now obsolete papers, because they have been stored together, can be tossed all together in one quick motion. Notice again that the file folder is used only as a labeling device. The pile of papers sits on top because it is unnecessary and inefficient to open the file folder and place the papers inside.

Fast and Furious Tip: Stacking trays are useful for holding *distinct* projects (one per tray!) with lots of paper-work to which you refer often. These are the papers that are used too frequently and retrieved too often to make filing them an efficient system.

After

The Active Basket

On the other side of the desk in the After photo to the left is a black "active" basket for "active papers." These are papers that have to do with this month's calendar. Here we find the invitation and directions to the wedding at the end of the month, notes for the call you're going to make to the doctor tomorrow, this month's church bulletin with service times, next week's school fieldtrip information packet, and the form you're still working on but wanted off of your desktop while you went to make dinner.

Slash folders in the "active" basket corral a handful of papers for near-term activities that will soon end. Ongoing long-term projects with dozens of papers go into the project stacking trays.

The "active" basket isn't deep—forcing you to weed it just about monthly (at which time most of its contents will be obsolete). The width must be a good 8 inches to accommodate an 8.5 x 11-inch paper, but the height shouldn't exceed 5 to 6 inches. Thus the paper is supported enough to stand upright but the top is still visible, and all the papers are easy to flip through without having to remove anything. In this same basket, I urge my clients to dump their calendar and their address book, both of which are referred to just about daily.

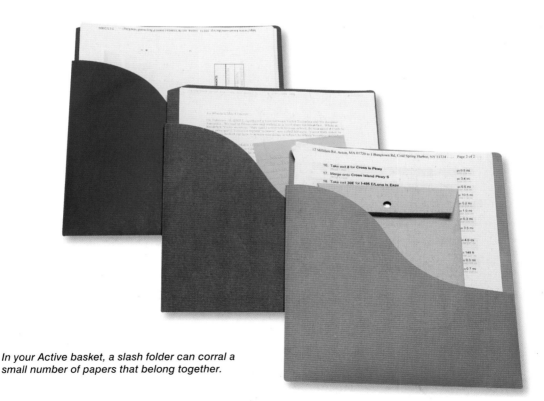

In your Active basket, a slash folder can corral a small number of papers that belong together.

Some activities require more than one paper. Two or three papers can just be stapled together, but to corral larger numbers and keep them together within the "active" basket, use colored slash folders. For example, you might want to use a slash folder to hold all your Girl Scout's information, such as an events sheet, directions to the campground, packing list, and ongoing badge paperwork. All of it is current, all of it is active, and it is easier to access and put away if it's together in a colored slash folder.

The "active" basket works because it's simple—one stop retrieval, one stop filing. Unless a project is large (encompassing dozens of papers) and ongoing (requiring its own project stacking tray), the paperwork is here. Papers that you rarely access go in file drawers. When you clear your desk at night, the paper you're working on gets dumped into the "active" basket.

THREE CONTAINERS FOR YOUR THREE TYPES OF PAPERWORK

1. **Active basket:** current papers that will become obsolete by the end of the month. Slash folders corral subjects that have more than one paper.

2. **Stacking tray:** ongoing individual current projects that have a large number of papers.

3. **File drawers:** papers that you rarely need to reference and archival files.

The Calendar

In the office "active" basket, a 3-ring binder with clear sheets like the one shown below holds all of the family's seasonal and yearlong schedules. The school calendar, the dance-school calendar, the soccer schedule, and so on all go into this folder. The plastic sheets, although a little fussy, are sturdier and more efficient than messing with a three-hole punch. Monthly bulletins or newsletters containing a calendar of current events—like the monthly church news bulletin—go in the active basket.

A binder with plastic sheeting gathers all the schedules and calendars—school, sports, activities—handy and together in your "active" basket.

The yearly binder may also contain a "seasonal schedule" prepared from a computer template. The schedule allows the family to refer to the *fixed* events of any given day. For instance, "Mattie Dance Class 3:00–4:00" might be printed on Tuesday of the Autumn Schedule. Note that the seasonal schedule is *not* meant for doctor's appointments, weddings, or any other *singular* events. These should be noted on the family calendar. Rather, the seasonal schedule is a quick reference aid for the first few weeks of any semester until new classes and other fixed activities are memorized. When seasons or activities change, the schedule can be updated accordingly and a new version printed for the binder, stapled to the family calendar, pinned on the bulletin board, taped to the wall, or posted in any busy, easy-to-access area until you've memorized the times and dates of all the activities. Such a schedule is probably unnecessary for a singleton or a couple, but in a busy family with multiple activities, it can be a lifesaver.

Fast and Furious Tip: If you have the space, you may want to pin all of your yearlong calendars, like the school holidays calendar, to a bulletin board above the desk instead of placing them in a binder. This is an even more efficient, if slightly less tidy-looking, approach than using a binder.

Office Supplies

Office supplies are also containerized for ease of access and ease to put away. In the photo here, you can see that a pencil cup with scissors and a stapler are left out and available. You'll also want a small container on the desktop, on a nearby shelf, or in the top desk drawer to hold a few rubber bands, some paperclips, and tape. In this same drawer, you'll need to keep a box of refill staples and a modest inventory of office supplies—a single pad of Post-it notes, a calculator, and so on—that you frequently use.

Avoid purchasing jumbo packs of office supplies that overwhelm your office storage.

As we look at our finished office in the After photo on page 159, we see a space that is comfortable, restful, and efficient. By simplifying our systems to fewer files, easily accessed boxes, and stacking trays, we have made it easy and convenient to process paperwork. But more importantly, by valuing efficiency over preparedness, by trying to keep only what we *know* we will need rather than everything we *might* need, by rejecting false economies of "sales" that seduce us into buying things we don't yet need, and by removing quickly and efficiently without shredding, we have reduced the number of papers in this office to a simple and manageable level.

> **Fast and Furious Tip:** Place your checkbook, a book of stamps, and some envelopes together in one "bill paying" space. Gathering these items and placing them together in a drawer at a desk and/or a cubby near the kitchen office and mail-sorting center will make your life much easier.

CHAPTER 9

THE KITCHEN

Before

THE KITCHEN is often the most heavily used room in any home. Mail, homework, coats, and purchases inevitably get dropped there. It's host to preparation, consumption, and cleanup of three meals and many snacks per day; it's also often where the family socializes. It's no wonder the kitchen is often called "the heart of the home."

But all this activity also means that the kitchen can be a clutter magnet. And if the kitchen is poorly organized, our chances of staying on top of the clutter are poorer still. In the Before photo shown here, you can see a typical kitchen belonging to a busy family of four. It is an averagely well organized kitchen in that it can and is used to cook and serve meals daily. But in our attempt to get this kitchen from average to clutter-free, we're going to have to weed, set some boundaries, and reorganize for no-fuss efficiency. Our goal is to create a no-fuss kitchen where snacks and lighter meals take less than a handful of minutes to clean, and even dinner requires no more than ten minutes to clear away and clean up.

In this chapter, we'll look at some of the common challenges in the kitchen and see how some fast and furious no-fuss organizing techniques can transform this room into an easy-to-maintain, restful, and efficient space.

After

HOW TO CREATE A PRACTICAL, NO-FUSS KITCHEN OFFICE

Let's begin our kitchen organization project by addressing the largest boundary violation taking place in this kitchen. Look at the Before photo below and ask yourself: What lives in this kitchen that doesn't belong here, that has nothing to do with food prep, food service, or dining? If you answered "papers," you're already thinking like an organizer.

Keeping papers out of the kitchen and food out of the office will forever simplify your life.

Papers don't belong in the kitchen. If you have to organize and clean away your papers every time you have to cook, it makes cooking that much harder. And if you have to clean the dirty dishes off the paperwork every time you want to pay your bills, it's likely that you'll fall behind in your bill paying.

Before

I urge every homeowner to set up an office separate from the kitchen. That being said, some families can never get out of the habit of dropping their schoolwork, newspapers, and mail on the kitchen counter. If this is the case with your family, don't just abandon the concept of a boundary; instead, make a boundary *within* the kitchen.

Because no one can relax through a major kitchen organization project if possibly important papers are being shuffled about, we began our kitchen reorganization by addressing the papers. This project followed our five fast and furious, no-fuss steps. Let's see how we took our kitchen office from the Before photo shown here to an efficient, organized space.

Fast and Furious Tip: Designate an isolated spot for your kitchen office: Isolation creates a *de facto* boundary.

THE KITCHEN OFFICE

STEP ONE

We began by scheduling three hours to tackle the kitchen papers. Because we hoped to see all the papers organized before tackling the rest of the kitchen, we allowed time for all five steps within the kitchen papers project.

STEP TWO

On the scheduled day, we began by weeding and sorting the kitchen papers. Many papers were deemed obsolete and ended up in the recycling bin. Books were weeded down to a few keeper cookbooks, the rest were either put in a donation bag or in piles earmarked for the bedrooms of their respective owners. The remaining paperwork was sorted by type into piles, and the piles themselves designated as either "office" or "kitchen." The homeowner defined "kitchen" papers as the "day-to-day" papers—the mail, the family calendar, the kids' school papers, and the newspaper.

STEP THREE

Next we removed the "office" paperwork—specifically the bills, financial paperwork, and large projects—and relocated it to the computer desk area in the office down the hall. Books made their way to the rooms where they belonged, and a small bag of book donations was taken out to the car.

STEP FOUR

We then named an area to create boundaries for the new kitchen office that was large enough to accommodate everything needed to process the day-to-day paperwork. In this particular kitchen, the small counter between the refrigerator and the dining room door, shown in the Before photo on the previous page was selected as our mini-office. We chose this spot because it was isolated from the food prep area. A large drawer below the counter was also drafted for our office area. The counter was cleared of kitchen items, and the drawer was emptied of its inefficient stack of heavy ceramic bowls.

STEP FIVE

Once the area was emptied and swiped out with a damp rag, it was clear that we would need some containers to create a mini kitchen office. With a little cannibalizing from other rooms, along with a quick trip to the office supply store, we were able to quickly set up an inexpensive, no-fuss, functional mini kitchen office (shown in the After photo on previous page).

To start, we placed a set of stacking trays on the counter to serve as a mail-sorting station. On each tray, we inserted easy-to-distinguish colored folders, quickly marked with a felt-tipped pen to provide *labels* such as "bills to pay" or "statements." Although we designated bill *paying* as an office activity, mail sorting remained a kitchen task. Our system allows for mail to be easily sorted by flinging it quickly on top of (not in!) the folder—in the appropriate stacking tray. There it can linger, in a sorted organized vertical pile, until bill-paying day, when the homeowner grabs it on her way to the office.

We took the phone off the kitchen wall near the hallway and placed a desktop version in our mini-office area instead. A caddy holds a small selection of stationery supplies: tape, pens, pencils, markers, scissors, some Post-it Notes, and a stapler. Next to the caddy is an "active" basket (see page 181.) This basket holds all the paperwork that is in active use as well as this month's calendar, the address book, and a pad of paper for writing down phone messages or the day's grocery list.

We recognize that our fast and furiously established no-fuss kitchen office is not tremendously attractive. We've tried to mitigate its aesthetic challenges by using a nice wicker "active" basket and procuring a wooden, rather than a plastic, caddy. And while papers will never look attractive, at least when they are corralled in one spot and further organized in stacking trays and baskets, they don't look like clutter. For day-to-day living, the area is useful, efficient, practical, and attractive enough.

Fast and Furious Tip: When choosing a mail-sorting stacking tray, buy one more tray than you think you will need. Empty storage is an invaluable organizational tool. It stands as a ready resource to corral paperwork for short-term day-to-day projects, and it can be drafted as kind of interim staging area.

HIDING THE KITCHEN OFFICE

The large drawer below the kitchen office counter formerly held serving bowls, as shown in the Before photo here. We claimed this drawer as part of the kitchen office, replacing the bowls with a small number of items corralled in a basket, including a checkbook, envelopes, and stamps. Any office supplies that didn't fit in the office supply caddy—and that are often used at this location—are also kept in this drawer. This drawer also provides a convenient space for a fast and furious "stowing" of our countertop office, as shown in the After photo here, on those formal occasions when we want the kitchen to look its best. Because the drawer is located right beneath the office, and because it is large and empty enough to handle all of the office "equipment," it takes just five seconds to slip everything from the countertop into the drawer before company arrives.

We placed the bowls that used to be in this drawer in the cabinets near the kitchen table. (See the After photo on page 187.) By placing them next to the table, they provide a decorative touch and are a breeze to put away—no need for laborious stacking!

If your children do their homework at the kitchen table, then maintain a convenient-to-the-table empty space like the one shown here so that they can quickly place their homework and homework supplies within when it is time to set the table for dinner.

HOW TO CREATE AN EFFICIENT RECYCLING SYSTEM

One of the greatest enemies of an organized home is an inconvenient waste removal system. Prior to our kitchen reorganization, the paper recycling basket in this kitchen sat on the opposite side of the table, far from the bulk of the paperwork. As shown in the Before photo below, the basket itself was so oversized that our homeowner could not possibly lift it. Extra, inefficient steps—bending down multiple times to empty the contents into a series of smaller bins or bags for transport to the curb—are tedious and time-consuming. Also, the basket's odd shape prevents the newspapers from lying neatly flat, creating an eyesore.

Our new bin, shown in the After photo below, is well shaped for the newspaper, and its wide handles make it easy to carry while its size and shape make it easy to empty in one simple motion. It has been moved from its remote location to a spot near the kitchen office so that junk mail can be conveniently dumped as the homeowners sort the mail. Younger children can leave graded school-work on the countertop in front of the kitchen office so that Mom and Dad can cast an eye over it before dropping it into the bin. (Older children should have their own homework designated recycling basket near their desk—see tip on page 75.) And when it's time to entertain, the bin can be shunted, fast and furiously, to a more hidden location (back alongside the table) in a matter of seconds.

Before

After

HOW TO CREATE A NO-FUSS PANTRY

It's odd to think of food as clutter, but if your food stores are dribbling out of your cupboards, or so packed into your cabinets you must move them around like chess pieces to see your stock, then you're flouting an important organizing principle: Inventory must conform to storage.

Let's look at some storage particulars by examining the Before and After photos of the pantry in this home. Organization started out well: The pantry is conveniently located next to the refrigerator, making it easy to check supplies. But the food shelves are so overcrowded that this family can't see what it already has, so duplicates get purchased.

> The most common cause of a stuffed and unwieldy food cabinet
> is the failure to make grocery lists.

It's also clear that one of the shoppers in this home doesn't adhere to a grocery list, continually buying favorites and sale items. So five boxes of popcorn are transformed from "foods we like" into clutter. Likewise, ten cans of on-sale mandarin oranges are costing the family valuable space and tying up capital that could be earning interest in the bank—talk about penny wise and pound foolish! Yet this family is not unusual; I see some version of their pantry in almost every home I enter. Let's see how applying our five fast and furious, no-fuss steps can turn this pantry around.

THE KITCHEN PANTRY

STEP ONE

Having addressed the paperwork, I suspected it would take roughly eight hours to get through the rest of this kitchen, starting with the pantry. We set aside two consecutive six-hour days to give ourselves plenty of wiggle room and container shopping time.

STEP TWO

So how do we take this pantry from stressful to organized? We begin with a fast and furious weeding. Keeper items were sorted into piles by type—snack foods, breakfast foods, and so on. The old and expired, mistakenly purchased, novelty foods, and no-longer-liked were either tossed or donated along with several redundancies. These were dropped in donation bags earmarked for the food pantry, along with serviceable-but-unnecessarily-large collections—in this case, paper goods and plastic wraps. Open boxes of food and open packages of paper goods along with an overstock of grocery bags were tossed without fussing about waste. Keeper food was sorted by type, and we kept the piles straight by labeling them with Post-it Notes.

> The limits and boundaries of your reorganization—that is to say, the names you designate for individual shelves and cupboards—will respond to your family's unique food preferences and lifestyle.

STEP THREE

Donations were taken to the car, and trash was taken to the garbage bins. Napkins, paper plates, blue plastic cups, and plastic silverware were also removed from this pantry and placed on the lower shelves of the cabinetry near the table where they will be used.

With removal complete, we gave the empty shelving a no-fuss "once over" with a damp sponge.

STEP FOUR

Perusing the size of our piles informed our new boundaries. We expanded the shelves dedicated to food and reduced the shelving for bags. Because there are many categories of food and four people living in this house, this was one of the few cases where I sometimes recommend not just naming the cabinets but using some quick, no-fuss labels—a felt-tipped marker and some stickers will do the job. Our names adhere to the system that we would find in any grocery store; there's no need to reinvent the wheel.

Food is arranged on the shelves so that every item is visible at a glance and easy to access. Nothing is stacked; nothing is hidden. This is possible only because we've tried to limit the inventory to that which will see this family through only until the next grocery trip. As for those duplicates the family just couldn't give up, we arranged them together front to back, so that when one is removed, more are immediately apparent.

STEP FIVE

With the pantry weeded, we realized that we needed only two containers for this space: a bin to corral some plastic grocery bags and a tool to organize the spices. These containers and a few others that we identified as we organized the rest of the room were either drafted from other parts of the house or purchased in one efficient shopping/donation-drop-off errand as the final step of our overall project. We'll discuss the containers in more detail as we look more closely at each shelf and drawer.

Fast and Furious Tip: The fast and furious method accepts a certain amount of "waste" because we recognize that the truly wasteful mistake was in acquiring too much. The money is already spent, and the effort and space to store overstock (or micromanage its journey to the perfect home) is still costing you. Donate what you can and trash the rest. Save the planet by committing, from this day forward, to acquiring only what you imminently need.

DON'T BE AFRAID TO RUN OUT OF THINGS

The fear of running low, of "not being prepared," is the perfectionist beast that sabotages many an organized home. Despite the dire warnings of the marketers and the prudence of your grandparents, who had to put up preserves if they hoped to eat produce through the winter months, overstocking on food in this modern age is the root, not the cure, for disorganization. A well organized home should *regularly run out of stock*! Putting a depleted item on the grocery list is an organizational triumph, indicating that you purchased a prudent amount while you avoided wasting space, time, and money storing the excess. Reliance on flexibility, resilience, and resourcefulness ("Oops, we are out of milk. Instead of cereal I guess I'll have some toast.") are the values that allow us to stock sensibly, promoting a simpler lifestyle while creating an organized home.

A pad of paper should sit permanently on the kitchen counter of every home for use as the running grocery list. The family member who goes to the grocery store can tear off the list when she goes, or if she forgets it, she can call home and ask for the list. A new list is begun the minute the old list has been removed.

In Depth: The Cereal and Breakfast Shelf

Looking at the reorganization in more detail, we start with the top shelf of the lower cabinet, shown in this Before photo. It seems that this shelf was probably originally a cereal and snack drawer. The snacks were thrown in willy-nilly because there were too many of them to fit in the drawer. The cereals were laid on their side and stacked—probably to accommodate their height and get more into the space available.

Although packing many things into a small space might *use* the space efficiently, it doesn't make *using* the space efficient. Boxes have to be unstacked and restacked if you want to get to the bottom cereal, and because you can't see the boxes on the bottom, some unstacking and shifting may be necessary just to see your options.

Efficiency of effort should take precedence over efficiency of space.

In the After photo, we see the results of weeding, sorting, and creating boundaries. Snacks have been removed from this shelf, and the names "cereals" and "breakfast foods" have given these items their own "homes," making them easy to find. Furthermore, all foods are arranged so that nothing is hidden, and every item on the shelf is visible, easy to remove, and easy to put away. The cereal has been unstacked, set upright or on its side, and arranged in such a way that all boxes are accessible without shifting others. The label boundaries of cereal and breakfast foods give an immediate sense of appropriate inventory.

We also see that any more than four or five cereal boxes will begin to intrude on the breakfast foods side of the cabinet, so a *de facto* limit has been set for the spectrum of cereal choices this family should have in a morning if they want to stay efficient and organized. Of course, another family might choose fewer cold cereals and more "breakfast foods." The limits and boundaries of your reorganization will correspond to your family's preferences and lifestyle.

As for the snacks, they have been weeded and given their own shelf above "baking." In this family, an entire shelf for snacks and treats fit their lifestyle.

FIVE TIPS TO KEEP YOUR CABINETS CLEAR AND YOUR WALLET AND BELLY FULL

1. Commit to eating what you've already purchased before purchasing more.

2. Keep an ongoing grocery list.

3. Shop only from the grocery list. (Purchase only those foods that you plan to eat before the next regularly scheduled trip to the grocery store.)

4. Don't worry about purchasing a meal for every night. For a five-day weeknight schedule, factor in one night for leftovers and another night for takeout.

5. Avoid bulk purchases. They clutter your cabinet with overstock.

In Depth: The Spice and Condiment Shelves

The second shelf in this pantry, shown in this Before photo, appears to have started out as the storage area for spices, oils, vinegars, and other condiments, but some snack foods, breakfast foods, and teas have invaded the space—probably because no one knew where else to put them. The most inefficient aspect of this drawer is the way it obscures the label of almost every spice container. I can just imagine that in hunting for the turmeric, I might have to fuss with a dozen or so bottles before laying my hands on the goal.

We moved the spices into a more fittingly proportioned drawer, and we weeded or relocated the rest of the food in the original drawer to its appropriately labeled shelf. Three identical salad dressings are probably too many to retain. They will certainly see the family through many months, but enough other food items have been weeded to allow for a couple areas of indulgence. You can see the results of our efforts in the After photo.

Fast and Furious Tip: Line up different varieties horizontally to display the options, but line up identical items vertically to show depth of stock.

Dried spices are at the peak of freshness for only about six months. As in so many homes, during the weeding process we disposed of an apothecary's worth of ancient spice bottles. Some were tossed because the family cook had taken to using small quantities of fresh spices from the produce department. A boundary was then created for the spices, in the form of a drawer to the left of the pantry, still in our food storage zone. Cloth napkins were removed from the drawer and an inexpensive, expandable plastic insert was purchased to instantly "containerize" the space. Now every spice can be seen in a single glance, as shown in the photo below. The spices are arranged in the drawer, labels showing, in *roughly* alphabetical order—a system everyone can understand.

Avoid organizing perfectionism in the spice drawer. Keeping jars roughly alphabetized is good enough.

In Depth: The Canned Goods Shelf

The third shelf started out as canned goods, but as this Before photo shows, you can barely *see* the cans under all the snacks. Weeding and naming again did the trick, leaving an organized no-fuss shelf (shown in the After photo), where all is visible, easy to stock, easy to take stock of, and easy to take stock away.

ARE THESE SHELVES *REALLY* REALISTIC?

On the day the photographer took these pictures of the pantry shelves, the art director asked, "Is this realistic? Can this family survive on this small amount of food?" This question reflects both the historical habits of the human race—when canning was necessary for "setting stores in for the winter"—and the brainwashing of a modern age.

This pantry holds five to six shelves of just carbohydrates. More carbohydrates, in the form of bread, are in a cabinet above the toaster. The other food groups and the bulk of the family's diet—the proteins, produce, and dairy—are in the refrigerator. The family lives five minutes from a grocery store and shops twice a week. So I ask you: Are *six* shelves of carbohydrates enough to see a family of four through three and a half days?

WHERE DID WE PUT THE BREAD AND COFFEE?

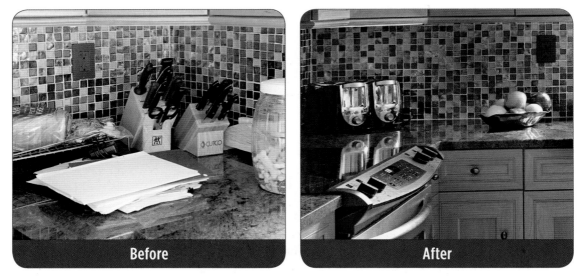

Before   After

Although our pantry area holds the bulk of the dry goods in this house, which makes it easy to check inventory before grocery shopping, there are two exceptions: the bread and the coffee.

In the Before photo shown here, you can see that prior to the reorganization, the bread was kept on the corner counter between the sink and stove because the family was concerned it would get crushed in the overcrowded pantry drawers. But the toaster and coffee maker were far from the sink and the bread, on the counter that has since been turned into the kitchen office.

In the After photo, you can see that the toaster has been relocated to the corner counter where the bread formerly resided. The coffee maker will have a home next to the toaster once an aesthetically pleasing stainless steel unit has been purchased.

The bread and coffee themselves are now stored in the corner cabinet just above the toaster and coffee maker (with the exception of one oversized container of coffee too large to fit in the corner cabinet—it remains in the pantry, on the "drinks" shelf until this overstock is used up). Because the family makes coffee and toast every morning, and because the coffee maker should be located next to the sink for easy cleaning, the bread, the coffee, and the coffee filters have been given a new home that gives precedence to everyday convenience. In this instance, boundaries have taken a backseat to the more important value of efficiency.

SMALL APPLIANCES, BIG CHALLENGE: HOW TO RECLAIM YOUR SPACE

Small appliances are massive space hogs in any kitchen, so challenge them for their right to be in yours. When was the last time you used the bread maker, pasta maker, or espresso machine? Do you prefer to fuss with a coffee grinder or buy ground beans at the store? If you got by without a rice cooker once, can you do so again? If you already have both a toaster and an oven, do you need a toaster oven?

> Two small appliances on the counter and two to three more in the cupboard should be more than sufficient in even the largest of homes.

In our spotlight home, this family made some wise decisions about boundaries that can serve as a good guide for the rest of us. They chose two small appliances to keep on the counter tops—the ones that are used daily (the toaster and coffee maker)—and three more (blender, food processor, mixer) to store in one of the lower cupboards, now called the "appliance cupboard." They donated the rice cooker and all other smaller appliances.

YOUR GRANDMA HAD IT RIGHT

Remember the anecdote from chapter 1 of the "gourmet" mother of three who hadn't cooked in her kitchen for eighteen months because every spare bit of counter space was taken up with expensive, ingenious, and useful kitchen products? The most important tool for cooking—counter space—had been sacrificed to specialty tools. If your grandmother could cook without all of these machines and specialty tools, so can you. Deprogram yourself from the new-age "cult of gadgets" and find some olde time religion. Pick the number of appliances that will *fit in your space* and rely on your resourcefulness to do without the rest.

HOW TO DEAL WITH DISHWARE

The location of the dishware cabinet in this house has been well chosen to hold many of the most often used dishes. Its close proximity to the dishwasher means that clean dishes can be put away in one simple motion without setting dishes on a counter for an interim period. Yet unloading the dishwasher will still require an inconvenience. As shown in the Before photo below left, the dishware is stacked and nested in such a way that one cannot avoid shifting one dish to remove or add another.

Why is this cabinet, while neat and clean, still such a cluttered space? Mostly because boundaries have been violated. Aside from dishware, the cabinet also holds a variety of other items: candy, decorative vases, medications, plastic water bottles, and plastic bowls and cups.

After weeding everything that isn't dishware, all of the most often used dishware was moved to this cabinet. The After photo shows that the cabinet is organized because every ceramic plate in each stack is the same as every other. There is never a reason to fuss with the top plate to get to the one underneath as they are all the same. And, of course, because they are the same, the stack is stable. If the children had been younger, this same scenario would have been created with plastic dishes.

Right: The newly organized cabinet makes so much sense that anyone from the homeowner's children to a visiting relative can unload the dishwasher into this cabinet with minimal instruction and in one simple motion.

Before

After

Notice also that every type of dishware has a boundary. There is a plate area, a bowl area, a mug area, and a most-often-used-wine-glasses area. There is no nesting, and adequate space has been left between dishware so that shifting is unnecessary.

Where Did the Items That We Took Out of the Cabinet Go?

The big change in the Before cabinet on page 206 is a result of weeding and setting boundaries. But where did all the stuff that we weeded out of the cabinet go?

Medications have been moved to their own small, appropriately sized shelf in a cabinet on the other side of the sink, as shown to the right. The shelf above the medication now holds a set of smaller glasses just about the right size to aid in pill taking. A simple shelf riser has been added to keep the medicines visible.

Before

After

Overflow water bottles and travel coffee mugs had previously been placed in the dishware cabinet after the water bottle drawer (shown in the Before photo to the left) got too full. To fit inventory to storage, the family pared down the water bottles to one per family member and the travel mugs to one per coffee/tea drinker. You can see the results of their paring in the After photo here. Of course, if you pare your travel mugs down to one per person, you'll have to bring the mug in from the car every night to wash it out for the next day. This is both efficient and prudent. Old cappuccino overturned in the car can forever leave a revolting smell and unsightly stain.

As for the rest of the extraneous items in the cabinet: The candy was tossed, some decorative dishware was moved to a glass-front cabinet, lesser valued items were donated, and old plasticware from the children's toddler days was recycled. The paper napkins were combined with the pack from the pantry and moved to a cabinet near the table. The paper muffin liners went into the pantry food shelf marked "baking," and the decorative tin and novelty fortune sticks were tossed.

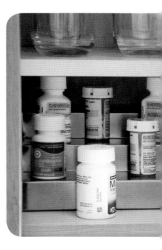

A shelf riser keeps stock in the back row up and visible.

Although novelty items can be fun the moment you first see them, after about a month, they lose their charm and morph into clutter. No joke can stand up to multiple retellings.

HOW TO FINE-TUNE YOUR FLATWARE DRAWER

Before | After

Flatware, like dishware, should be kept convenient to the dishwasher. Again, this family has wisely chosen just such a location. However, as you can see in this Before photo, the drawer itself has devolved into a cluttered space. The problem stems mostly from boundaries; the drawer holds items other than just flatware. The family decided to store non-flatware here because it is an extra large drawer, with enough space to hold something other than flatware. But because this extra space was not "named," it had become a catchall for all those little, seemingly indefinable items that so many people find themselves at a loss to organize.

Start by Weeding and Sorting

We started reorganizing the drawer by weeding out the non-flatware items first. The matches and twine, for instance, would not be found in the flatware section of a store; they would be found in the hardware section. In our homes, the hardware section is a utility closet, a kitchen utility drawer (never a "junk" drawer or "miscellaneous" drawer!), or the basement work bench and utility shelves. In this case, we designated a kitchen drawer as the "utility" drawer (shown to the right) to hold the twine, matches, and a few tools (a small hammer, wrench, and screwdriver) for quick fixes. The matches were weeded down to three books, which are more than enough for a family that doesn't have a gas stove.

A mostly full box of generic birthday candles went into the pantry drawer with the baked goods; the large single-number candles were thrown out. Novelty measuring spoons, flatware, and tools were also thrown out or donated. Most of the serving pieces and cooking utensils, on the other hand, found homes with their brethren in a second, oversized "cooking utensils" drawer. We also weeded out some of the wooden spoons. (How many wooden spoons does one family need? I commonly find as many as eight per household, when most of us could get by with two.) Similarly, one each of measuring spoons, spatulas, and slotted spoons should be sufficient, with a little resourcefulness and frequent use of the sink, to adequately service a household.

A utility drawer in the kitchen houses items such as twine, matches, and small tools.

AVOID KNIFE OVERLOAD

Many professional chefs use just one knife—a medium-sized chef's knife—for most of their kitchen activity, but cutlery companies try to convince us that a panoply of styles and sizes are necessary. Still, one knife would be a little stringent. I recommend six or seven at most. Two medium chef's knives, a couple of small paring knives, a large meat carving knife, a bread knife, and maybe one other specialty knife that responds to your family culture (oyster shuck? cleaver?) should be perfectly adequate.

Use Containers to Tame the Space

After weeding, there was still an extra space in the flatware tray. As you can see in the After photo on page 210, this family chose to fill this place with some wooden salad servers by dubbing them more tableware than cookware and because eliminating their bulk relieved pressure on the "cooking utensil" drawer. Another family might have chosen to place large serving spoons or corn-on-the-cob holders here. As long as that bin-within-the-tray is named and the objects within conform to that boundary (so that it doesn't become a "catchall"), organization is maintained. Because space was still available, the remaining knives were containerized in a drawer-insert cutlery knife block (purchased at a kitchenware store), while space to the left of the tray was given over to a bin to hold chopsticks.

HOW TO STOP A TUPPERWARE-STYLE TAKEOVER

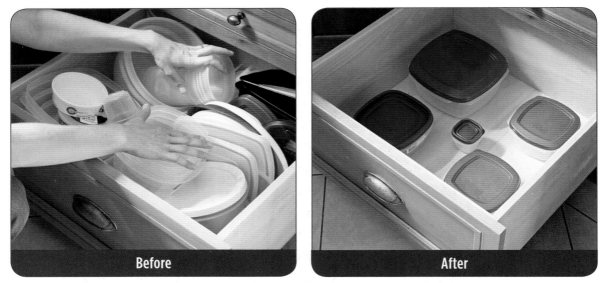

Before

After

In many homes, like this one, the "food storage container" drawer morphs into a labyrinthine plastic jungle. As you can see in this Before photo, to remove a container and its matching lid required un-nesting and major rifling. It is possible that only the homeowner would be able to make a match, though probably not quickly nor unfailingly. Furthermore, the drawer was so overloaded that half the time it required two hands to close it—one to push down the contents and the other to push the drawer closed.

A rational, no-fuss weeding provides the fastest fix for this drawer. We should retain enough food storage containers to see each of the family members who regularly pack a lunch through one day. Four separate containers will see us through two leftover courses for two dinners. By day three, the oldest leftovers should either be eaten or ready to toss, allowing us to reclaim those containers. For families who don't pack lunches, four to six plastic containers are sufficient. This family, whose members rarely pack a lunch but who regularly have leftovers, kept five containers. Three of these containers are the same size, further simplifying the matching of lids to correctly sized bottoms.

Running out of food storage containers keeps leftovers on our radar and encourages us to clean out the fridge.

BUT IS THIS ENOUGH?

Our family weeded so effectively that the containers can all be stored wearing their lids, forever eliminating the inefficient "great lid hunt." But is this enough? The companies who sell these products would like you to believe that you are not organized if a small drumstick rolls around in a larger container, or if you must split the stuffing between two medium-sized containers, but you know better. Organization isn't created by always matching any possible volume of leftovers to a perfectly sized container. Organization is achieved by limiting containers to a manageable number and getting resourceful with the stock at hand.

One of my favorite organizational truisms is "if you have leftover Tupperware after a holiday meal, you have too much Tupperware!" It is more efficient to occasionally get resourceful with plastic wrap and foil than to wrestle *daily* with myriad lids and toppling piles.

HOW TO PUT A LID ON THOSE POTS—ONCE AND FOR ALL

Before

After

Let's look at one final project that can be completed simply by weeding. This family's cookware drawer is large, roomy, and conveniently located next to the sink. Yet as you can see in this Before photo, it is still difficult to remove a pot from, or return a pot to, this drawer. The culprit is overstock.

A LITTLE FLEXIBILITY GOES A LONG WAY

If you are a crêpe maker plying your living in the heart of Paris, you'll need a specialty crêpe pan. If you spend your mornings pulling lobsters off the dock in the North Atlantic so that you can serve them up in your roadside lobster shack, you'll need an enormous lobster pot. But the rest of us will reap untold organizational benefits if we can be flexible enough about the density of our pancake to resourcefully make do with a fry pan, and phlegmatic enough about the size and variety of our stew pots to switch the menu from lobsters to chili if we want to feed dozens.

Even Julia Child wouldn't need this many redundant pots.

When we sorted "like with like," we found that despite slight variations, and with the exception of the waffle iron, there are multiple redundancies of three types of pot: the fry pan or skillet, saucepan, and large stew pot. The average stove has only four burners, so how many pots can we ever really use at one time? With a little resourcefulness, you can definitely make a delicious, elegant meal with six pots or less. Even if you make a meal that requires three skillets, there is a good chance that at least two of those courses will be sequential, so you'll have an opportunity to rinse out a skillet. Or just maybe you'll get resourceful and draft the larger saucepan for the job.

Once we pare down the number of pots, every pot can be stored with its lid. Like the Tupperware drawer, we have forever eliminated the great lid safari. And because this drawer now has adequate room, anyone—including the seven-year-old child, mother-in-law, and informal dinner guests—can put the pots away when the dishwashing is done.

ONE FINAL LOOK

Before

After

Let's take one more look at our Before and After kitchen shown in the photos above. Although the family may have less "stuff" in their new, weeded kitchen, overall they will find it easier to use. Why? Because they'll have more counter space to prepare meals, more cupboard space so dish retrieval and return is a breeze, and more pantry space so it's easy to see their stores and efficiently make a grocery list and plan meals. By reducing their volume of possessions and eliminating unnecessary steps, they have decimated an enemy army whose weapons are the many small inefficiencies that bedevil an organized life.

CONCLUSION

YOU'VE LEARNED THE FIVE NO-FUSS STEPS that are a part of every organizing project. You've seen how a fast and furious, no-fuss approach—one that rejects perfectionism, micro-frugality, and over-preparedness—can create an efficient and organized home. You've watched as we used these steps and this method to organize real homes, allowing for small indulgences along the way. All that is left is for *you* to apply these steps and this method to your own spaces and home. You can find the beauty that comes with clean, the peace that comes with organized, the sentiments that come from living in the now, and the contentment to be found in "good enough." I wish you the best of luck as you change your life and set off on your own organizing adventures!

With a fast and furious five-step attack and a no-fuss battle cry of "efficiency!" you can reclaim your space, your time, and your life.

ACKNOWLEDGEMENTS

FIRST AND FOREMOST I WOULD LIKE TO THANK Shannon K. LeMay-Finn, my developmental editor. Her sure and gentle editorial hand helped shape and strengthen this work. No author could ask for a more deft and able partner to share, shoulder, and lighten the load. Thank you as well to John Gettings and Amanda Waddell at Fair Winds Press. John had the vision, and Amanda set me on my journey, saw me through a few false starts and blind alleys, and with patient support made sure I found my way through. I would also like to express my appreciation to the creative team and staff at Fair Winds: Sylvia McArdle, whose expertise kept things sane, Jennifer Bright Reich and Tiffany Hill, whose efforts smoothed the rough edges, and Tara Connelly, whose warm hospitality was very much appreciated.

There are those outside the publishing world to whom I must express my great indebtedness. Thank you to Julie Jankelson, M.D., and Diane and Marty Krasnick for lending a helping hand. To Amy Cerel, whose boundless generosity, quiet support, and unfaltering kindness immeasurably enriched both the book and my life this past year, please know that you have my heartfelt gratitude. And, of course, to Kristin Leary, whose unwavering belief sowed the seeds of my success: I owe you more than I can say. And finally, to my clients, I thank you for opening your homes and lives to me. This book would not have been possible without your courageous decision to share your journey.

When one person in a family works all day and writes all night, every other family member is forced to pick up the slack, and so it was with my family this past year. I would like to thank my mother, Marcia Waters, who has informed so much of my work. To my daughter Esther, who fed and fetched her little sister and helped out with her grandmother, thank you my dear. Hannah, my sweet, as always you do what needs to be done with grace and good sense so I can work and not worry; you can never know how much I appreciate you. And Leah, my darling, you stepped up to the plate and parented yourself this past year. Thank you for your flexibility, your resilience, and your good humor through it all. And finally, to my beloved husband, David, who kept the whole ship afloat, no thanks could ever, will ever, be enough.

ABOUT THE AUTHOR

SUSAN C. PINSKY is the founder of the professional organizing service Organizationally Yours (www.organizationallyours.com) and author of *Organizing Solutions for People with Attention Deficit Disorder* (Fair Winds Press, 2006). She can be seen frequently in public speaking engagements and on television and radio stations around the country as a commentator and advisor on organizational issues. She is a member of the National Association of Professional Organizers and a graduate of Wellesley College.

Susan lives in Acton, Massachusetts, with her husband and three children.